Herman Lindqvist

A Journey Through Swedish History

Translation: Alan Tapsell

Principle sponsor
for the project
The Swedish History:
AB Tipstjänst

Photo: Sören Hallgren
Peter Segermark

Nordiska museet and Statens Historiska Museum
in collaboration with the Regional Museums,
Bra Böcker and AB Tipstjänst

Project Management

Sten Rentzhog, *Project Manager, Museum Director*
Tel: +46 63 127125

Statens Historiska museum
Tel: +46 8 7839400
Box 5405
114 84 Stockholm
Ulf Erik Hagberg, *museum director*
Lars Andersson, *exhibition director*

Nordiska Museet
Tel: +46 8 6664600
Box 27820
115 93 Stockholm
Agne Furingsten, *museum director*
Berit Rönnstedt, *exhibition director*

Caroline Virgin-Björkman,
director of communications
Address:
Den Svenska Historien
Box 27820
115 93 Stocholm
Tel: +46 8 6664600
Fax: +46 8 6664601

Organizing Museums:
Statens Historiska Museum, Stockholm
Nordiska museet, Stockholm

Co-Organizing Museums:
Stockholms läns museum, Stockholm
Upplandsmuseet, Uppsala
Södermanlands museum, Nyköping
Östergötlands länsmuseum, Linköping
Jönköpings läns museum, Jönköping
Smålands museum, Växjö
Kalmar läns museum, Kalmar
Länsmuseet Gotlands fornsal, Visby
Blekinge läns museum, Karlskrona
Kristianstads läns museum, Kristianstad
Kulturen, Lund
Hallands länsmuseer, Varberg och Halmstad
Bohusläns museum, Uddevalla
Älvsborgs Länsmuseum, Vänersborg
Skaraborgs länsmuseum, Skara
Värmlands Museum, Karlstad
Örebro läns museum, Örebro
Västmanlands läns museum, Västerås
Dalarnas museum, Falun
Länsmuseet i Gävleborgs län, Gävle
Jämtlands läns museum, Östersund
Västerbottens museum, Umeå
Norrbottens museum, Luleå

Collaborating Museums:
Sundsvalls museum, Sundsvall
Arbetets museum, Norrköping
Göteborgs historiska museum, Göteborg
Malmö museer, Malmö

Preface

During 1993 and 1994 there was a joint exhibition, Swedish History, at the National Historical Museum and the Nordic Museum, in Stockholm. Here visitors could follow the course of Sweden's history from earliest times until today, acquainting themselves with the fascinating cavalcade of events which have formed the background of modern Sweden.

In an endeavour to enhance the drama of all this we asked the historian Herman Lindqvist to study the exhibition at both museums and describe how and what he experienced.

The purpose of this venture was to promote history as a vital and essential factor in our lives. Our national heritage is founded on a common language and history and if we are to understand our society today then we must be able to review it in terms of the past.

A great many of our problems today are a result of having lost contact with the past. It is like being astray in the woods; having forgotten which way we have come. It is not enough to look behind us five steps or five years. In order to know where we are and find our way ahead it is essential that we have a proper idea of what has gone before.

This knowledge and understanding of the past ought not to be restricted to professional historians, instead it should be accessible to us all, whatever our background. That was the object of this project; to enable each and every one of us to rediscover our history and in this way learn to appreciate how Sweden became what she is today.

If history really is to become the province of us all and not merely of the specialized few, then we must create a new, more open and democratic approach to the subject than hitherto.

One way of making history more approachable is by presenting each successive period and its people against a background of the conditions and values of those times; we must be able to envisage those periods and re-live them. We have to discard many of the established accounts of history with all the presumptuousness, condescending irony and superior comparisons between our age and other times and ideals.

Another means of making history accessible is to allow past events to speak for themselves; to permit people to discover for themselves what actually happened, instead of insisting that they content themselves with analyses and explanations, which inevitably vary according to current social viewpoints and attitudes. It is not until we have a proper knowledge of, and insight into events as they really were that we can justifiably attempt to interpret them.

It is not necessary that everyone construes history in the same way. More important is that we can all enjoy access to the vast treasure trove of impressions and experience which history has to offer; that each and every one of us according to our requirements and values can fashion a satisfying concept of our past.

Sten Rentzhog

Museum director,
project manager for
A JOURNEY THROUGH SWEDISH HISTORY

Dynasties and chieftaindoms

In this picture stone from Häggeby in Uppland an early artist depicts a stallion-baiting scene. The horse was once a sacred animal, associated with the god Frey.

The earliest "documents" we have are picture stones from Gotland, up to 1500 years old. They described the feats of gods and chieftains, but also how people lived and what their weapons and ships looked like.

The "Golden Helmet" from a chieftain's grave in Vendel was a ceremonial headpiece made by one of the great masters of the time. Helmets by the same craftsman have been discovered in England

Our excursion through Sweden's history which will bring us ultimately to the Sweden of today, begins at the royal burial mounds in Old Uppsala. The period is 400–500 AD, the late Iron Age – a mere 60 generations back in time.

Here one could witness human and animal sacrifices when a chieftain was cremated and interred at Old Uppsala, the hub of the Svear realm.

In the central farming settlements certain families had attained greater wealth than others and the heads of these families became local chieftains. When a cheiftain died his body was burned on a pyre and he was interred beneath a mound. Some of the largest of these burial mounds are here in Old Uppsala.

They were raised alongside each other, like the Egyptian pyramids, and for the same purpose: to demonstrate the continuity of power and the affinity between kings and gods. The principal Aesir temple was located close by.

Ancient chronicles claim that it was the Svear kings Aun the Old, his son Egil Tunnadolg and Egil's grandson Adils the Powerful who are entombed in the three Old Uppsala mounds, though there is no proper historical evidence of this. Theirs were farming and seafaring folk who had early made contact with other peoples.

Those objects interred with the early kings and chieftains were symbols of power and status, often of foreign manufacture or made by immigrant craftsmen, for example the splendid ceremonial helmets and armour from the graves of the chieftains in Vendel and Valsgärde. These graves are likewise in Uppland though they are later than the Old Uppsala mounds. Weapons fashioned by the same Vendel craftsman have been found in the graves of early English kings. For fourteen generations, right up until the 11th century, the Vendel chieftains were interred in their ships without first being cremated, which is why their weapons and other regalia have been unearthed in such a good state of preservation.

Out in Europe the great migrations were going on. In Svealand and Götaland and on the islands of Gotland and Öland there was also unrest which is apparent even today from the many ruins of early strongholds.

At that time most of the inhabitants of Sweden were Germanic, speaking a language which would one day become Swedish. Many of them had the same names as we use in Sweden today: Björn, Ulf, Sten and Karl. The women's names were Åsa, Inga, Tove, Sigrid or Gunnel. But the word *Sverige* (Sweden) was still unheard of and the country was called *Svitjod*. The deities were the warrior god Oden, the thunder and rain god Thor and the fertility god Frö or Frey.

Ansgar and Birka

The expeditions of the Svear southwards were not always peaceful trading missions. In the early 9th century news spread across Britain and along the French and Dutch coastlines of the coming of the fierce seafarers from the north. They landed from their fast, shallow-draught craft to ravage, plunder and burn even among the churches and monasteries. The Vikings had arrived.

The memory of these invaders still lives in the minds of the people of Europe, for the Vikings are one of the few features of Scandinavian history familiar to most Europeans.

There must have been a tremendous eruption of acitivity in Scandinavia when among a population of little more than 800 000 there was a sufficient number of young, seafaring warriors to attain so much in a few decades: they overran a large part of Britain (*Bretland*) and of Ire-

The Birka Crucifix, made in silver over 1000 years ago, is Sweden's oldest portrayal of Christ.

Birka was Sweden's first real town, a meeting place for merchants from both near and far. Here Swedish goods were bartered for foreign weapons, glass work and jewellery. Possibly as many as 2 000 people lived permanently in Birka.

land where they founded a kingdom. They discovered Iceland and Greenland, they passed the winter on Newfoundland and fought with the local natives (*skrälingar*). They founded another kingdom in northern France (Normandy) and yet another in Russia. They navigated the Russian rivers to the Black Sea and the Caspian Sea. They reached the Byzantine capital of Constantinople (*Miklagård*) where hundreds of them did service in the emperor's personal guard and they pressed on to the Caliphate's Baghdad (*Särkland*). They returned again and again to harass London, burn Hamburg and threaten Paris and Lisbon. They sailed through the straits of Gibraltar, sold slaves in Morocco (*Blåland*) and stormed Seville and Mallorca.

It was on account of the ill-deeds of these Vikings that in the summer of 830 the 20-year old Benedictine monk Ansgar from Amiens came to Birka on a small island in Lake Mälar only a few miles to the west of modern Stockholm. He had been dispatched by the Frankish emperor Louis the Pious with instructions to pacify these wild Northerners.

King Björn of the Svear was not entirely opposed to this since through Christendom he could make contact with leading political and trading powers in Europe, which would be good for business. According to Ansgar's chronicles the Svear voted on this at the *Ting*. Ansgar triumphed and the first Christian church, or chapel, was built at Birka.

The mission made but slow progress and few permitted themselves to be baptized. Ansgar probably worked mainly with serfs and prisoners-of-war who already were Christians. After a few years he left Birka but returned in 852. Meanwhile the astute tradesmen with a nose for the demands of the time began making moulds for casting both Thor hammers and Christian crosses. Thus Christendom and the Aesir cult thrived side by side in the "open city" of Birka.

Birka, on the island of Björkö in Lake Mälar, was Sweden's first town. Excavations are still going on there today and finds disclose that Birka was a sort of rendezvous for merchants from many lands. There was a barter trade here: Swedish furs, dried fish, serfs and prisoners-of-war in exchange for European gold, silver and iron work, jewellery and ornaments, weapons, glass and ceramics. There can have been as many as 2 000 inhabitants in Birka, more than in many of Sweden's later, mediaeval towns.

Several thousand Swedish runestones describe briefly and succinctly the exploits of the Vikings, though also the lives and destinies of those who remained at home. There are over twenty stones telling the story of the last-known major voyage, Ingvar Vittfarne's fateful expedition all the way to the Caspian Sea when most of his men perished en route. Our first Christian cross and our first prayers are also inscribed on runestones.

Pagan Cults

It must have been a bewildering time for the people of *Svitjod*. While the first church bells, often with runic inscriptions, summoned them to church in Götaland, farther up in Uppland the Aesir folk still listened to the thunder of Thor's chariots roaring across the heavens while his great hammer forged lightning over the horizon. Meantime Odin's fateful ravens, Hugin and Munin, flapped in with ill-omened news.

The Aesirs intensified their activities in Old Uppsala, the temple was renovated and Frey became increasingly prominent. He was now known as "God of the World" and was paid tribute to for the blessings of fertility, abundant crops and sensual pleasures. The Frey cult contained distinct sexual elements and the oldest extant Christian record from the land of the Svear, Adam of Bremen's chronicle, describes how the statue of Frey had an immense phallus.

Every nine years when the *disablot*, the ancient Nordic sacrificial festival, took place in Old Uppsala there was growing disquiet. People came in from near and far and the Svear king personally conducted the sacrificial rites when living animals and humans were hanged from the sacred tree adjoining the temple. Nine males of each species were sacrificed: nine men, nine stallions, nine dogs. . .

Ansgar's successor in Birka was murdered, but new missionaries continued to arrive from various parts. They came from the archbishop of the Frankish kings in Hamburg, from Norway, from the Danish Viking king in England, possibly also from the east; from Greek-Orthodox Russia.

According to legend the English monks Sigfrid and David were sent to Västergötland. Botvid, probably Swedish though of English instruction, came to Södermanland along with the Englishman Eskil. Stefan came from Hamburg to work in Hälsingland. They all died martyr's deaths, Eskil in Tuna which thereby became Eskilstuna and Botvid in Södertörn, hence Botkyrka.

By this time everything must have been turned upsidedown for these Norherners. Many of them perhaps interpreted it as a prelude to *Ragnarök*, the Twilight of the Gods; the world's end as the Aesirs had foretold. The giants and the gods would fight their last great battle when all mankind, including the giants and the gods themselves, would perish.

And yet out of all this there emerged nevertheless a new, more peaceful world. The people forsook their old deities and in time not even the Svear kings would attend the temple sacrifices. This was the advent of a new era with strange music and new sensibilities. Another world was opening before them.

Pagan and Christian cult symbols. The figure, top left, is a image of the god Frey from Rällinge in Södermanland.

Christianity

The churches were adorned with madonna sculptures in wood. One of these is Maria from Mosjö in Närke. This was carved some 900 years ago by one of the English missionaries active in and around Rekarne (south of Lake Mälar).

No one knows exactly how or when it came about, but Olof Skötkonung is believed to have been the first king in Sweden to become a Christian. He reigned ca. 995–1022. Bishop Adam of Bremen later recorded that it was the English monk Sigfrid who baptized Olof Skötkonung and his entire family in the Husaby spring at Kinnekulle, in Västergötland. Immediately afterwards the king ordered the building of a timber stave-church, probably of the same type as the 900-year old church from Hemse on Gotland the outer walls of which are now in the Museum of History, Stockholm. Olof Skötkonung also installed Sweden's first bishop, Turgot, who made his residence "in the big town of Skara", as Adam of Bremen described it.

According to the records Olof Skötkonung ruled over both Svear and Goths. Thus by about the year 1000 these kingdoms had been united and we had come one step closer to the formation of a Swedish nation. Olof's realm was a sort of federation of independent provinces with their own laws, though ruled over by one Christian king. Strangers from other provinces were regarded as foreigners, which was probably the origin of today's strong sense of provincial solidarity.

In an endeavour to eliminate paganism and the reactionary forces in Old Uppsala and evoke the spirit of a new era Olof Skötkonung's father, Erik Segersäll, had already earlier founded a new royal town, Sigtuna. Now Olof recruited English minters to make the first Swedish coins.

Yet as the runestones record, the country was still called *Svitjod* and the Old Uppsala temple long outlived Olof Skötkonung.

According to ancient and historically uncertain royal records it was the ninth king after Olof Skötkonung, Inge the Elder, who put down the last Aesir revolt which was led by Inge's own brother-in-law, known as Blot-Sven. The Uppsala temple was destroyed and the ancient sacrificial tree was cut down to the roots. Nothing was allowed to remain. This is believed to have happened around the year 1087.

Adam of Bremen records that a Christian church was very quickly built on the site of the former pagan temple. The Aesir gods had been defeated. Thus the Holy Roman Catholic Church finally emerged triumphant in Sweden 200 years after the arrival of Ansgar on Björkö in Lake Mälar.

Nevertheless pagan customs and practices persisted and the third, fourth, fifth and sixth days of the week are in modern Swedish still named after the gods Tyr, Oden, Thor and Frigg who was the wife of Oden. And the Christian churches have been built at places the names of which are still reminiscent of the old gods and other customs: Frövi (where the god Frö or Frey was worshipped), Frösön (after Frey), Ulleråker and Ullevi (after Ull), Onsala and Odensala (Oden's hall).

The roman catholic church

With the coming of the new religion Sweden became one of the last countries in Europe to be integrated in European culture. This was thanks to the priests and monks from England, Germany and France who brought in their manuscripts and books and introduced medical science, building techniques and new tools and implements.

Churches were built in stone, loftier and more grand than the earlier timbered chapels. Stain glass windows illustrated the stories of the Bible in radiant colours. These fine churches in Skara and Sigtuna echoed with the same hymns and prayers as those in Rome and Paris. Monks and nuns read and taught from the same Latin books in Linköping and Eskilstuna as did their brothers and sisters in Worms and Bologna. In this way, thanks to the Church, Sweden became part of a European community which would endure for 400 years. The Romanesque style was introduced at an early stage as can be seen, for example, from the Nordic-crafted Broddetorp altar, the most splendid mediaeval altarpiece in the country.

The first monastery was built by Cistercian monks who brought with them medicinal herbs and new cultivation methods. They settled in Alvastra in Östergötland and at Nydala in Småland. Later the monasteries of Varnhem in Västergötland, Julita in Södermanland and Roma on Gotland were founded.

Parishes now began to grow up around the rural stone churches. (The word *socken* – parish – derives from the verb *söka* – to seek; all those who sought to join the same church belonged to the same parish). Admittedly these local people often received help and ideas from elsewhere, but they built their churches themselves, using techniques they had never previously employed and they built them loftier and larger altogether than anything they had seen before. The parish church constructed in stone was an enormous project of hitherto unheard of proportions. The whole of Scandinavia belonged to one and the same ecclesiastical province, Dacia. In the beginning the principal Swedish bishop had his episcopal see in Skara while the archbishop of the overall Dacia province was resident in Danish Lund.

In the middle of the 12th century the Svear kings turned their attention to Finland. According to Erik's Chronicle in the 1150's Erik Jevardsson led a crusade against southwestern Finland where parts of the population had long been Swedish and many were doubtless already Christian. He built the first Åbo castle and cathedral and left the English monk Henrik behind as Finland's first bishop.

Erik Jevardsson was murdered in Östra Aros, now Uppsala, around 1160. His son created a martyr legend around him and he was soon being worshipped as a saint, Erik the Holy, though Rome never acknowledged him as a true saint. Nevertheless throughout the Middle

The first stone churches were regarded as amazing structures in the villages where hitherto there had existed only small, timbered buildings. These churches were adorned with crucifixes and statuettes of the saints, in Romanesque style. God the Father sits before a gilded copper altarpiece with the Gospel on his knee, blessing the congregation. This altarpiece was in the Broddetorp church which has since been demolished, one of the 500 mediaeval churches in Sweden's oldest diocese, Skara. Such a costly altarpiece may well have been commissioned originally for the early cathedral in Skara.

Ages there were pilgrimages to his relics in Uppsala cathedral. During springtime the casket in which these relics were preserved was borne forth in procession with supplications for a good harvest. In this way the Erik cult became a sort of continuation of the ancient Frey cult of the Svear. Erik the Holy became Sweden's first patron saint. Bishop Henrik also died a martyr's death in Turku and in his turn became Finland's first patron saint.

The Swedish military and crusading expeditions against the militant Greek-Orthodox Novgorods in eastern Finland continued. Birger Jarl seized Tavastland in the 1240's and built the first Tavastehus fortress. In the 1290's Torgils Knutsson took Karelia and founded Viborg before continuing even farther east to build the Landskrona fortress at the mouth of the Neva.

Thus Finland, which in the Middle Ages was called *Österland* (Eastland), became part of Sweden in the same way that Norrland (today's northern Sweden) was successively incorporated in the realm.

Sweden had now become a broad, east-to-west Roman Catholic country or, to quote Erik's Chronicle:

This land it was all Christian and I
believe the Russian king had missed it. . .

All the king's men

We are now at the end of the 13th century. After a bitter life and death struggle between four brothers, in 1275 Sweden was ruled by Magnus Ladulås, son of Birger Jarl of the Folkunga dynasty. This family reigned for four generations, from 1250 to 1364, one of the most brilliant yet at the same time most woeful periods in Sweden's history.

A new order emerged, like a pyramid with the king, nobles and priesthood at the top and at the base the common people who paid all the taxes and were required to labour for king and nobles.

Pictures and sculptures in the churches reflect the roles of those in power during the Middle Ages. The king sits on his throne, elevated and armed. His authority is divine and he is crowned by a bishop. St George the knight preserves and protects the social order.

An entirely new order emerged. This can be likened to a pyramid: at the apex the king, nobles and priesthood none of whom were burdened by taxes. Below these was a new class, the urban burghers, and below these again the common pople; 95 % of the population who lived in the rural areas and struggled to survive as smallholders, fishermen and hunters. It was this great mass at the bottom of the pyramid who paid all the taxes and duties and who were forced to do day-work for king and nobles.

Three events created the structure of this pyramid. The first was the battle of Sparrsätra in 1247 when the final resistance to royal despotism and taxation was crushed. The Sigtuna annals afterwards commented resignedly: "In this year of 1247 at Sparrsätra did the common folk lose victory and liberty and were required to provide grain and diverse other imposts."

In the following year, 1248, a legate appeared from the Vatican and at a meeting in Skänninge it was decreed that the churches, priesthood and monasteries would be answerable only to the Pope, not to the king. No taxes whatsoever would be imposed on the Church.

New combat and weapon techniques with heavily armoured knights demanded a new military organization at greater cost to the king. So the taxation system had to be revised.

The third major event which helped create this mediaeval social pyramid was the assembly of Magnus Ladulås's diet on the island of Alsnö outside Stockholm in 1280 when the temporal lords were created. Those who served their king with mounted soldiers need pay no taxes. This decree produced a new social class: the nobility.

The fallen warriors were Gotland peasants who were cut down by Danish knights in 1361

This was Sweden's Age of Chivalry with ideas brought in from France. Here a knight should not only be skilled in combat according to all the rules of chivalry, he should also know how to hunt with falcons, write verse, court the ladies with ballads, and play chess. Our Swedish "knights" were perhaps not always as gallant as they should have been. But they were good combatants, and could play chess too, as is evident from their sets of chessmen in the Museum of History.

The sons of the influential began as squires and if they proved able could be knighted with the right to be addressed as "Herr". Only the wife of a knight was entitled to call herself "Fru". The knights had their coats-of-arms emblazoned on their shields and these devices were later adopted as surnames: Natt och Dag, Bielke, Sparre.

Regular diets were now held, the forerunners of our modern *Riksdag* or parliament. The new nobles around the king became the first counsellors of the realm, a body which in due course would become the government. These first counsellors of the realm were the bishops and the heads of the most eminent families.

But the law still differed in different parts of the country. Every province had its own set of laws which the *lagman*, i.e. the local lawman or legislator, had been required to know by heart. But now these laws were recorded in order to strenghten further the central authority. These written laws became Sweden's first book, the Early Västgöta Statutes, ca. 1280.

For the purpose of collecting taxes, furthering trade and keeping an eye on landowners and peasants alike, the first towns and national strongholds were now built. The most important town was Stockholm. From its central location the king could control his realm both east and west of the Baltic Sea.

At this time and during subsequent decades new towns were founded and mendicant monasteries were built or enlarged, for example Arboga, Nyköping, Söderköping, Enköping, Västerås, Jönköping, Kalmar, Linköping, Norrköping, Gamleby-Västervik, Uppsala, Vadstena, Örebro and Visby on Gotland, also Turku (Åbo), Tavastehus, Borgå and Viborg, all in "*Österland*", i.e. in Finland.

The towns

Most of the houses were wooden; small and humble. The main trading towns were laid out on the German pattern; the town square was in the middle surrounded by the church, the townhall, the better shops and the dwellings of the wealthier merchants.

Periodically German immigrants dominated trading activities in the Swedish towns. It was Germans from the Hanse cities who conducted practically all the export business and who for long periods owned more than 40 % of the stone houses in Stockholm. There were times when the Swedes were little more than a protected minority in their own towns and a law had to be passed whereby not more than half the mayors and half the councillors should be German. Swedes should also have a say in matters in their own town!

The Germany influence was everywhere, even in the language. Thus today we still use such Low German words as *stad* (town), *borgmästare* (mayor) and *rådhus* (town/cityhall). But there are also many

The mediaeval towns were small with narrow, crooked streets. Merchants, often called in from Germany, conducted the commerce. The townfolk kept their own cows and pigs and the alleyways stank of waste water. At the beginning of the Middle Ages Sweden had one town only, but by the end of this period there were 45 or more! A further 25 towns sprang up in provinces which were then still Danish or Norwegian possessions.

Stockholm's oldest seal, from 1296.

Örebro's seal, from 1331.

other extant words revealing the strong German influence in the late Middle Ages: *köpman* (merchant), *slaktare* (butcher), *skräddare* (tailor), *kosta* (cost), *mynt* (coin), *socker* (sugar), *fängelse* (prison). The townfolk also added their own words and the Stockholm vocabulary now began to develop.

And in the parish records new, un-Swedish names were appearing: Herman, Henrik, Konrad and Gertrud.

The ordinary town dwellings were low and similar to those in the rural areas. Most of them had a stable or small barn since many kept a cow, and they would have some sort of little workshop and perhaps a stall facing the street for selling things. Many also owned a bit of arable land somewhere near the city gates. Goats grazed on the turf roofs. For a long time the only stone or brick buildings were the church and the strongholds and possibly also a monastery.

There was a stank in the alleyways since all waste matter was thrown into the street, giving the pigs something to grub about in. The more respectable streets were laid with planks and later cobblestones.

The peasants had to come into town to sell and buy. Practically all trading was forbidden in the countryside. If there was a monastery then there were usually some sort of primitive hospital facilities. The monks or nuns could be both French and German.

The narrow alleyways were crowded with country and townfolk. Finns, not then foreigners for their capital, too, was Stockholm, were beginning to come in, selling fish and other goods and many of them settled here. In town the peasants could sell their own produce and find new tools or buy salt, spices and foreign cloth, and maybe drink imported beers of which there were at least six different brews in the taverns. One could also pay a visit to the municipal bathhouse which was to be found in every town, likewise an inn to accommodate travellers. Alongside the coastal town quays, cogs from Lübeck, Rostock or Holland were tied up, unloading or loading. Another prominent feature here might be the big iron-scales used for weighing the Bergslagen products to be shipped down to the continent.

No foreign merchant was allowed to pass through the city gates without paying a duty on his goods. There could be divergent weights and measures in different towns or provinces so that everything was weighed and measured according to local standards. At night the gates were closed and no one was permitted either to enter or to leave.

One of the most important mediaeval towns was Nyköping where Magnus Ladulås resided in his newly-built Nyköpingshus, a place which will always be associated with a particularly lurid period in Sweden's history.

This drama began when the king died 1290. He was the first king to be interred in the Franciscan monks' newly-built sanctuary – today's Riddarholm church, which became the burial place for most Swedish kings.

The Nyköping banquet, 1317

It is the widow of Magnus Ladulås, Countess Helvig of Holstein, who can tell this sorrowful story. She came to Sweden as a 14-year old bride and was the first queen to be crowned here, an event to be remembered, especially in Söderköping for that town burned to the ground during the festivities. This in its way was an omen of what was to come. Queen Helvig became a widow at the early age of 28.

She was to live through the death of five of her six children and all her close relations by disease, mortal combat and murder before she herself died at the age of 64.

William Shakespeare could scarcely have done better. Here were all the ingredients of tragedy. Three brothers, ambitious and ruthless: Birger who inherited the throne, his brother Erik, Duke of Södermanland whom Erik's Chronicle describes as "handsome to behold, noble was he and courteous, brave in danger", and the youngest brother Valdemar, Duke of Finland.

Then there were their wives, royal daughters who were young, ambitious women, and brutal warriors and conniving courtiers.

The rivalry between the brothers was nurtured by a series of complex intrigues which sometimes erupted into physical violence, occasionally followed by reconciliation celebrations where it was safest to keep one hand on the hilt of your weapon.

In 1306 the two younger brothers attended a feast held by King Birger at Håtuna. In the middle of the night accompanied by an armed band the two younger brothers rushed into the royal apartment and attempted to seize the king, his queen and their son. The son contrived to escape in the tumult but Birger and his queen were trapped and fettered.

Now Erik would become king of Sweden – or so he thought.

War followed. Birger's supporters, the Danish and Norwegian kings and German princes joined the fray. They were nearly all related in one way or another.

Meanwhile for the peasants in Västergötland and southern Sweden the Håtuna incident had serious consequences since for several years the fighting continued across their homesteads and farmlands. Ultimately Erik was compelled to release Birger and his queen, Sweden was divided into three parts and Erik established his own kingdom in western Sweden.

Erik and Valdemar married each his own princess in Oslo. Erik's consort, Ingeborg, was but 11 years old. In due course they each bore a son and Ingeborg's was named Magnus.

There then followed some years of tension while King Birger brooded over his plans for revenge. The final reckoning came at Christmas 1317. Birger invited his brothers to a great banquet at Nyköpingshus,

Shakespeare could scarcely have done better. The final reckoning among the Folkunga brothers, the Håtuna incident and the Nyköping banquet, were monstrous events. But had all this not happened Sweden may have been permanently separated into three mediaeval small kingdoms.

"Mead and wine were in plenty", comments Erik's Chronicle. "They danced in and they danced out", added a Danish account.

That night after the festivities finally came to an end Birger's men broke in on the unsuspecting younger brothers and put them in chains. Erik and Valdemar, half-naked, beaten and bruised were then lowered, chains and all, through a trapdoor into the deepest dungeon in the prison tower, whereafter, according to the Chronicle, Birger cried down to them: "Remember Håtuna, well this will be the worse for you."

Birger believed that Sweden would now once more become a united kingdom. But there was civil war anew and the king was forced to flee, having first, says the Chronicle, thrown the key to the dungeon in the moat. The starved corpses of Erik and Valdemar were not recovered until the following year. Erik's Chronicle describes how with the help of a boar's tusk they had managed to dig their way through half the dungeon wall before they expired.

King Birger died in exile and his son was imprisoned and executed. The only conceivable heir remaining was Erik's infant son Magnus who had just inherited the whole of Norway. He was but three years old when he was elected king of Sweden.

What, meanwhile, would Scandinavia have looked like today if there had been no Nyköping banquet? If the three brothers had all survived and 14th century Sweden had been effectively divided up into three separate, independent kingdoms?

Magnus Eriksson, 1316–1374

The 3-years old Magnus Eriksson, king of Norway, was now elected king of Sweden. This was the beginning of a long and brilliant reign which coincided with Sweden's mediaeval golden age. His life, however, was to end in tragedy, in the stormy waters of a Norwegian fjord.

No Swedish monarch has ever reigned as long as Magnus Eriksson, 46 years during which time he achieved so much, yet ultimately lost everything. At one time his was the biggest realm in Europe, extending from Karelia in the east to Greenland in the west, from the North Cape in the north down to the Öresund in the south. He was entitled king of Sweden, Norway and Scania, having succeeded in purchasing the provinces of Scania and Blekinge from Danmark.

At midsummer 1319 the 3-years old Magnus Eriksson was placed on the Mora Stone outside Uppsala to be endowed with the kingdom of Sweden. Far left: At a meeting in Kalmar in 1332, when Magnus came of age, he purchased Scania for 34 000 marks in silver. Near left: In 1335 he toured the Mälar and Vättern regions and it was then that he composed his renowned decree abolishing thralldom.

When he became of age Magnus embarked on the *Eriksgata*, the traditional tour of the realm when each province swore allegiance to the monarch. In Skara in 1335 he wrote the famous edict abolishing thralldom throughout Sweden.

At the age of 18 he married a French count's daughter, Blanche of Namur from the royal house of Artois. Blanche bore him two sons, Erik and Håkan.

Important events took place in the realm. The first *landslag*, the national law code, was drawn up and this applied to each and every province. The first chapter here prescribed how the royal appointments should proceed, how the *Eriksgata* should be conducted and how the Council of the Realm should be organized. The *landslag* was, then, in effect, Sweden's first form of government.

The first coins were minted with the Three Crowns device, and in 1359 during a grave political crisis, a national assembly was called for at Kalmar. This summoned not only members of the Council of the Realm and the Church but also "elected representatives from every market town and four men from each and every *landsaga*" (lawman's domain). What this amounted to was the very first assembly of representatives from the four Estates. In fact for various reasons the Kalmar assembly never did take place, but it was nevertheless a first attempt.

Yet all that had begun so promisingly ended in the final tragedy of the Folkunga dynasty.

Because of his debts the king was forced to mortgage a great deal of the Crown lands to the big landowners. He also became involved in disputes with the nobles and Church. A rebellion broke out and the king's own son took the dissidents' part.

In the midst of all this the plague struck Sweden and at the same time the struggle for power continued until the counsellors and both the king's sons compelled Magnus Eriksson to divide up the realm. His son Håkan had inherited Norway while in time Erik acquired most of the provinces in Sweden and the whole of Finland. Then abruptly Erik and his entire family died.

Left: Magnus Eriksson drew up a national law code applicable to all the rural regions, and a municipal law code for the towns. These remained in force for almost 400 years.

Right: Magnus's eldest son, Erik, led a rebellion against his father and the king was forced to yield. At a meeting in Jönköping in 1337 Sweden was divided between father and sons into three kingdoms.

In the ensuing confusion the Danish king, Valdemar Atterdag first seized Scania, Blekinge and Halland and then the islands of Öland and Gotland. Magnus Eriksson was deposed and Håkan was elected king of both Sweden and Norway. It was then that King Håkan issued a decree whereby Finland, or "Eastland", was granted its own lawman and the right to participate in the election of the king. The province of Finland was thereby formally accorded the same status as the other provinces of the realm.

Magnus and Håkan were unexpectedly reconciliated and allied themselves with their former arch-enemy Valdemar Atterdag. Håkan married Valdemar's 10-years old daughter Margareta. This was too much for some of the nobles. They organized a revolt, seized the important town of Stockholm and Kalmar and arranged for Magnus's nephew Albrekt of Mecklenberg to be elected king. Magnus was put in irons in Stockholm palace where he remained for six years before he was finally able to make off to join his son Håkan in Norway.

This prolonged drama finally drew to a close when Magnus Eriksson, then sixty years old, perished in a shipwreck off Norway in 1374.

The Plague

Before the coming of the plague there were wild rumours followed by fear and panic. Those who were able sought refuge elsewhere. The Swedes were warned. There was no lack of omens and portents in the sky for those who could interpret them. Others needed only listen to the stories of the fugitives from stricken towns.

The Black Death began in China in 1333 and twelve years later it reached Europe, via the Crimea where the Tartars and Christians were fighting each other. This was the first example ever of biological warfare when the Tartar commander beseiged and bombarded the town of Kaffa with the corpses of soldiers and rats killed by the plague. They were hurled in by the Tartars' ballistas. Kaffa was an important trading point between China and Europe and the disease was brought in from the East along the silk routes. Kaffa soon fell by these macabre tactics and the plague then was spread by ship westward to Europe.

It came to Bergen in Norway in 1349 on an English vessel, the crew of which were all dying or dead. By the following year it had reached Sweden in its various forms. People in their dirty, overcrowded dwellings were unable to protect themselves against the infection which was carried mainly by black rat fleas.

It was generally concluded that the plague was God's punishment for the sins of the people, just as King Magnus Eriksson explained in a royal decree where he exhorted his subjects to do penance ande pray. Church bells were tolled and the people embarked on religious pilgrimages. Many fasted and made generous donations to churches and monasteries. Others scourged themselves. Sorceresses muttered their incantations and primitive apothecaries brewed strange potions, while others resorted to a new medicine, *brännvin* or aquavit.

According to certain, much-disputed calculations one third of Sweden's population perished during the plague. The population in 1350 was reckoned at about 500 000 and had this been today then 2 ½ million people would have died.

Whatever did or did not happen during the years of the plague, however, the shock of the calamity was so great that stories were told for generations afterwards; legends of how Death stalked across the country and where in some places but a single individual survived. There was said to have been great piles of corpses in the alleyways of Stockholm, farms and villages were abandoned throughout the land, livestock died and farming declined and ceased.

The fear, the suffering and the death that struck large areas of Europe even more so than in Sweden is revealed in the Church art of the time so that the Age of Chivalry's brave and dignified Christ figure on the cross becomes instead a distorted, tormented son of God.

Possibly there was a "physician" in the monasteries. But most people had to cope as best they could. The majority were convinced it was divine punishment and that prayers, pilgrimages and penance were the only possible salvation. The plague physicians believed they could cheat death by wearing "beaks" that filtered the air they breathed through a filling of aromatic herbs.

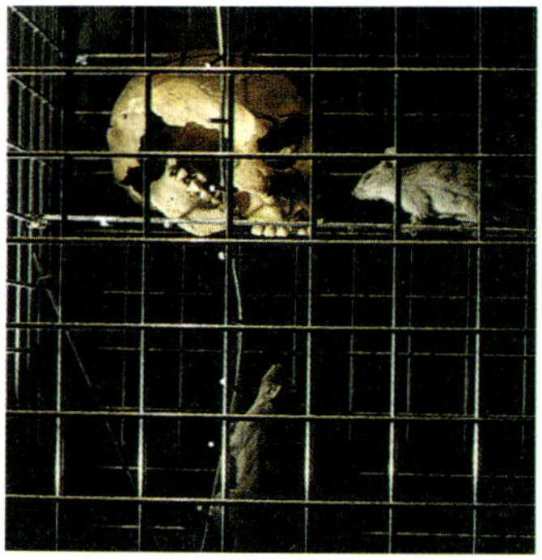

St. Bridget, 1303–1373

She became the only Swedish saint recognized by Rome. This magnificent ceremony took place in the Vatican on October 7, 1391.

Right up until the Reformation pilgims came to Vadstena from all over Scandinavia and parts of Europe to pay homage to St. Bridget, to study there or to seek help at the celebrated hospital in the convent.

Every year on St. Bridget's Day, October 7, thousands of candles are lighted in churches throughout the Catholic world, honouring Sweden's one lasting contribution to European culture and the first Swede to become renowned beyond our frontiers.

There exist no contemporary portraits of St. Bridget. This is one of the many later sculptures of her, fashioned in wood, from the parish of Länna in Uppland.

She called herself the princess of Närke when she arrived in Rome; a princess in a hair shirt and homespun cloth.

She knew the world, had seen everything. She had visited Europe's most important shrines at that time. The most powerful men in Sweden had frequented her childhood home, related to the royal household, she had served at court and her father, husband and sons were all lawmen and counsellors of the realm. She kept company with queens and cardinals.

Yet often at the same time she worked among prostitutes and the sick and the poor.

She preached humility and obedience, though never hesitated herself to assail or scold whomsoever she considered merited it: pope or monk, king or bailiff.

At a time when not even the daughters of great men in the realm could read or write she produced a multitude of scripts, more than 800 over the years, which were translated into the principal languages of mediaeval Europe and are still regarded as major literary works from that time.

She founded her own monastic organization even though she was never herself a nun, and that organization still exists 600 years later.

The convent in Vadstena became Sweden's cultural centre, maintaining contact with Europe's leading universities and monasteries. Books and manuscripts circulated among them and were copied. The Vadstena convent library became the largest in Scandinavia with over one thousand volumes. Here zealous nuns and monks created Sweden's first written language.

The strength and inspiration for all this, declared Bridget, came from above, in revelations from God.

The Kalmar union, 1397

Scandinavia suddenly emerged from obscurity. Popes, emperors and other leaders became aware that a Nordic realm had been created which was larger than any other in Europe.

This was a union which extended from Iceland in the north to Germany in the south, from Karelia in the east to the remaining Viking colonies on Greenland in the west. In addition the Faroes, the Shetlands and the Orkneys were part of this realm.

The queen was Margareta, daughter of Valdemar Atterdag of Denmark. At the age of ten she had been married off to Magnus Eriksson's son, Håkan, who ruled Norway. By the time she was 34 her husband and young son had died, while she had contrived to take over both Denmark and Norway. When the Swedish nobles and counsellors of the realm revolted against Albrekt of Mecklenburg's excessively pro-German rule in Sweden, they called upon Margareta for assistance. She came with Danish and Norwegian troops. Albrekt who referred scornfully to Margareta as King Trouserless, was defeated in the field, imprisoned and finally expelled from the realm. Margareta was then elected queen of Sweden, in 1389.

She was the first queen ever to reign in Sweden.

Margareta was entirely Scandinavian: raised in Sweden, Danish father, Norwegian mother and a Swedish spouse. St. Bridget's daughter Märta Ulfsdotter had been responsible for her education and upbringing.

This vast realm, the Nordic union, could not be ignored either by the European powers or by Rome. That is one of the reasons why Bridget was canonized just at this time. The new great power should be honoured with its own saint.

Queen Margareta was our first sovereign to develop her own universal political visions. Her idea was that the Nordic countries should become a consolidated unit with a common defence and foreign policy.

The countries involved would come to each other's aid in the event of war in the region, while at the same time by the terms of the union these countries would not engage in armed conflict among themselves. The sovereign would have at her or his side counsellors of the realm from each of the three kingdoms, while each kingdom would be governed by its own officials and laws. Altogether the Nordic region was a powerful bloc against the menacing German states and Hanse. For the Swedish folk in general things would remain much the same as before, but for the lords, especially those in the south, the union offered major economic advantages.

The decision to create a union was made at a meeting in Kalmar in July 1397 where representatives of the three kingdoms had assembled.

The Nordic union was bigger than any other realm in Europe, extending from Karelia to Greenland; from the North Cape to the frontiers of the German kingdoms in the south. Denmark had the largest population and was the wealthiest and politically most important of the three kingdoms and thus the union was governed by Denmark's Queen Margareta. She was herself an able politician and saw the union as a defensive bloc against the powerful Hanseatic League. The union was formed in 1397 and survived in varying degree until the 1520's.

Erik of Pomerania (right) is portrayed here with two early 15th century emperors: Erik's cousin, the German emperor Sigismund, and the Byzantine emperor Johannes. Erik's Nordic union kingdom embraced large areas of northern Europe. Through family connections in England and South Germany Erik sought to hold in check the Hanseatic League's economic dominance in the North.

At this same time Margareta appointed her successor. After the death of her son she lacked an heir so she had made her sister's son, Erik of Pomerania, her foster-son. At the union meeting Erik was crowned king of Sweden. He was then 15-years old and had already the year before sworn the royal oath in good Danish at Uppsala. Meanwhile Margareta continued to govern the union until her death in 1412.

Margareta's vision survived and functioned for 50 years and this was our longest period of peace throughout the Middle Ages. Sweden was, in fact, involved in wars but these were beyond the frontiers of the union. Altogether the union was to survive for yet another hundred years though during that time there was widespread internal strife before it was finally dissolved after the Stockholm bloodbath of 1521.

Denmark with three quarters of a million inhabitants was the leading nation, culturally and economically. Sweden which still had not become a national state but was rather a federation of provinces, had about a half million inhabitants, Norway a quarter of a million. In these circumstances and with the strong Danish links through Margareta and Erik of Pomerania, Denmark became the predominant power within the union, something which in time was to have grave consequences.

What would have happened if the union had continued to function? Would the three Scandinavian countries all be speaking the same language today? Would we have had a Danish monarch? And how would we have managed in the world wars?

…KT REBELLION

…mer Eve 1434. Angry miners and
…liff's residence in Borganäs, near
…the insurrection spread across the
…kt Engelbrektsson.
…ghout Europe. The peasantry had re-
…d Bohemia. Now it was Sweden's turn.
…n in just Bergslagen, Dalarna? This region
… industrial proletariat: miners and those who
…nd foundries. Iron and copper were shipped out
…to Europe through German merchants and mine-
…ad been settled in Bergslagen for centuries.
…ere hard times for the common people. There was very little
…iable and new taxes to be paid. Meanwhile the iron could not
…hipped out because of war in the Baltic, isolating Sweden. Unem-
…loyment spread and the king's bailiffs increased their pressure; the people must be made to pay their taxes. The most detested official of all was the Danish bailiff, Jösse Eriksson.

Then came the eruption. Engelbrekt Engelbrektsson was about 40 years old, a short, powerfully-built miner of German extraction. He was a member of the lesser nobility with interests in the mining business. As a young, well-born man he had probably had some experience of war since from the very beginning of the rebellion he emerged as an able organizer, strategist and leader.

His peasant army moved off with spiked clubs, axes and flaming torches, led by mounted noblemen. Within a few months a great many bailiff residences had been burned to the ground.

The purpose of the miners and the peasants was to rid themselves of the worst of the bailiffs, to have the unjust taxes abolished and to be able to move out the Bergslagen iron again. They were in no way opposed to the union as such. Neither were they in any way nationalists, for Sweden had not yet become a national state. They were fighting for Bergslagen and for their own wellbeing. Yet their revolt has since come to be regarded as Sweden's first struggle for liberty.

The more successful Engelbrekt and his followers were, the more people joined him from all sectors of the community. The ultimate victory came in August 1434 when the counsellors of the realm, that is to say the government, met with Engelbrekt in the town of Vadstena.

And if there were any doubt in the minds of these counsellors they had only to look out of the window. There was gathered a menacing assembly of peasants formidably armed with cudgels and staves. Thus the counsellors there and then renounced their allegiance to the king, probably assuming they could utilize this situation to their own advantage and acquire more power.

This handsome statue in wood of Karl Knutsson Bonde came from the studio of the renowned sculptor Bengt Notke. It was made in 1480 and the original is in Gripsholm castle. The exhibition's copy in stone is from the Bonde chapel in Spånga church.

Between 1448 and 1480 Karl Knutsson Bonde was three times king of Sweden and once king of Norway. The kneeling king seen here was originally part of Notke's St George and the Dragon group. The composite coat-of-arms at his waist incorporates the coats-of-arms of Sweden and Norway with the Bonde family device in the centre.

King Erik conce
Promises were broke
tilities ensued. Engelb
a meeting in Arboga du
this has been called our
ment, since representati
levels of the community
Engelbrekt was now appo
rikshövitsman, i.e. a captain
realm, and also a counsellor
realm. He was granted lifetime te
cy of Örebro castle while his sec
in-command, the young Karl Knu
son Bonde became *rikets marsk*, Lor
High Constable of the Realm, in other words commander of the army.

Now as the lord of Örebro Engelbrekt was presumably content with what he had achieved. The worst of the bailiffs had been disposed of, the king had agreed to abide by the laws of the country and taxes were to be reduced.

But national unrest erupted again and again during the winter of 1436. Engelbrekt led the fighting in southern Sweden. On April 27 he set out on a journey to Stockholm. His party was waylaid and Engelbrekt was murdered by the young Måns Bengtsson. This was to some extent an internal affair between these two, but the lords of the realm apparently approved the deed. Engelbrekt and his followers were no longer needed, the lords had achieved their ends. The assassin was never apprehended.

Two years later King Erik was deposed and he withdrew to Gotland were he survived for many years as a privateer. The next king, Christopher of Bavaria, reigned for only a few year before he died and he was succeeded by Karl Knutsson Bonde, who became unique in being elected king of Sweden three times.

ᑊD ITS IRON

vith their dark mines and glowing
ːzed the first rebellion in Sweden.
ːrtant element in national politics
, in Stockholm were compelled to

ı iron, Sweden's very first major export
ı produced in many parts of the country but
ı an abundance of ore as in Bergslagen which at
. areas of three provinces: Västmanland, Dalarna

and Värmland. Iron production had begun early here, possibly as far back as the late 12th century, long before the first Germans made their appearance in Bergslagen.

One of the oldest blast-furnaces in the country is *Lapphyttan* near Norberg in Västmanland. Iron production in Norberg is mentioned on a parchment dated 1303, but archeologists have discovered that iron has been produced here without interruption for 800 years. The last blast-furnace was extinguished in Dannemora, Bergslagen, as recently as 1992.

Producing iron required a lot of labour. People were needed down in the mines, they were needed out in the forests felling trees to feed the furnaces and they were needed to operate the waterwheels. Others had to keep the furnaces burning and process the white-hot metal. To recruit this labour it was decreed that felons would be granted some form of pardon in Bergslagen if they would agree to work in the mines. Bergslagen had its own laws, its own system of justice and its own courts.

Engelbrekt's followers came from the mines and foundries of Bergslagen because this was the only region where there existed a form of industrial proletariat. Iron has been produced in Bergslagen for over 800 years. A lot of labour was needed in the forests, mines and foundries and for this reason those recruited here had certain special privileges. The foundries were built by running water so that the blast-furnace bellows could be powered by waterwheels. The rock face was fired and then chilled to split the rock before the ore could be broken. Iron exports from Sweden began as early as the 13th century.

The ore in the ground was the property of the Crown, but the peasants who owned this land set up their own iron and copper cooperative, jointly owning and operating their own mines, foundries or blast-furnaces. They acquired their privileges for all this from the king and they worked season by season, farming their land and mining their ore.

However there was often a demand for more labour than could be obtained voluntarily and then they rounded up vagrants and any other generally homeless individuals for forced labour in the mines.

This policy resulted in a constant turnover of an often very rough clientele who were in no way tied down to farming and these became Sweden's first industrial proletariat.

It was mainly to protect themselves against this sort of unruly element that the mining people were granted the right to carry weapons, a privilege which in due time was to have a certain influence on Sweden's history.

Earlier, even back in the 13th century, German experts, including Engelbrekt's forebears, had come to Bergslagen, as is indicated by such place names as Saxhyttan and Saxåhyttan. Other names like Garphyttan and Garpenberg suggest that the German immigrants were perhaps not too popular, since in Sweden during the Middle Ages *garp* meant a German braggart or bully. But it was the Hanse merchants, from Lübeck in particular, who organized the iron export trade and invested in new foundries and mines.

The mining and export of copper also began during the early Middle Ages. At Kopparberget in Falun production was in full stride in the 1300's and in 1360 Magnus Eriksson proclaimed Sweden's first laws prescribing how the work should be organized. These consisted of detailed rules and regulations for the mining people – all in Latin!

The battle of Brunkeberg, 1471

The beginning of the end of the union with Denmark came on the morning of October 10, 1471. The Battle of Brunkeberg was a turning point in Swedish history.

Sweden was governed by the regent Sten Sture the Elder. Since the union had still not been dissolved Christian I arrived in Stockholm by ship to occupy the royal palace and reclaim his kingdom.

But Sten Sture and those who were opposed to the union were resolved to fight and took up their position along *Brunkebergsåsen*, a boulder ridge which ran in a north-south direction across what is today the centre of Stockholm.

What happened that day changed the course of history. This was described in simple terms as a battle between Danes and Swedish nationalists which Sweden won. That is an altogether *too* simple explanation however.

Sten Sture himself saw it as a contest between a knight and a dragon, and there is no doubt who the dragon was. Since then sober historians have stripped away the patriotic glamour which had gradually built up around this historic battle. It has since been discovered that Sten Sture had at his side not only the Stockholm merchants and the peasantry and miners from Bergslagen, but also the landlords with interests in foreign trade and the iron industry and, in addition, the border nobility who were anti-Danish.

And backing King Christian besides his Danes was "an alliance of landed gentry and peasants from the province of Uppland; the self-sufficient agrarian classes from the centre of the kingdom who up until this time had steered Sweden's destiny" (Lönnroth). Among the Swedes who fought for Christian I were members of the families which would later be called Oxenstierna and Vasa.

Christian was additionally aided by German and Scottish mercenaries.

The Swedish lords were concerned not so much with the freedom or otherwise of their country, but rather with their own economic and individual interests, especially Sten Sture the Elder.

It was a bitter battle which Sten Sture's wife Ingeborg and the mayor of Stockholm witnessed from the city wall. Finally the Swedish forces attacking from all sides set fire to the Danish fortifications and King Christian fled to his ship, bleeding and injured in the mouth. Afterwards the Brunkeberg ridge and Norrmalm were littered with more than 2 000 corpses, Swedes and Danes alike.

There was now a sort of national revival right across the country and Sweden began to become a nationalist state. Except for a short period from 1497 to 1501, for those in power in Sweden the union no longer existed and it was finally dissolved in 1523.

Bengt Notke's sculptural group of St. George and the dragon in Stockholm's Storkyrka *was unveiled on New Year's Eve, 1489. This is an allegory dedicated to the victory of Sten Sture and the Swedes over Christian I and his Danes in Stock holm. St. George is Sten Sture – his coat-of-arms can be seen on the hindquarters of the horse – the dragon is Denmark and the princess is Sweden. In the original, larger group the princess's father was also present in the guise of Sten Sture's uncle and predecessor Karl Knutsson Bonde.*

Detail showing a figure being crushed beneath the dragon's foot.

The Brunkeberg Battle day of victory, October 10 1471, long remained a national day of commemoration in Stockholm, celebrating the victory and paying homage to Sten Sture who himself commissioned the knight and dragon sculptural group now in *Storkyrkan*, Stockholm cathedral.

The victor was Sten Sture and very quickly with all the stratagem and energy of a Renaissance prince he removed each and every one who had ambitions to share his power. For 27 years Sten Sture ruled the country with a firm grip on those around him, though at the same time to the benefit of the common people. Few leaders have seized so many estates and farms as brutally as Sten Sture, but the only ones who suffered from this were the lords and the Church. For the common people there followed almost three decades without civil war. No peasant army was recruited and livestock and arable and pasture land was left in peace. No houses were burned down. The foundation was laid for a strong central administration and from this time onward the *Riksdag* met regularly with peasants and burghers. This was a unique situation in Europe, but as Sten Sture the Elder would often say:

That which concerns all should be assented by all.

Mediaeval enlightenment

The Middle Ages were by no means a dark age in Sweden's history. Rather this was a brilliant period when through the Catholic church Sweden enjoyed direct contact with Europe, and Renaissance Italy in particular.

All our culture, all our art and enlightenment came through the Church. The bishops, all of whom were Swedish, had to be accredited by Rome. These were powerful men. They attended the Council of the Realm, they had their own palaces and chiefdoms and their own armed units. They were mostly well-educated individuals who had received their university instruction in Bologna, Paris or Rostock.

The Church was very wealthy, it owned one farm in six throughout the country. The richest of all was the earliest diocese, Skara, where the bishop collected taxes from 3352 homesteads, compared with the bishop of Åbo's tax claims on a "mere" 643 homesteads.

The churches collected great treasures, splendid works in silver and gold which were brought forth for different occasions and ceremonies. During hard times, in war for instance, when the powers-that-were threatened the Church these treasures were secreted away. Some of this hidden treasure did not reappear until centuries later, as for example Linköping cathedral's silver collection which was probably buried by the last Catholic bishop Hans Brask in the early 16th century.

The cathedrals collected as many relics as possible, objects from

Bengt Notke's statue of the English archbishop and martyr Thomas Becket is from the Skepptuna church in Uppland.

The Middle Ages were a brilliant cultural era in Sweden's history. Below: a 16th century graduale *(hymnbook) written on parchment. Västerås cathedral.*

14th century drinking vessel in wood.

The Linköping treasure. From left: Holy Communion cup and a monstrance. Reliquariums in the form of a statuette of Catherine of Alexandria and forearms of the saints Eskil and Bridget.

One of the most magnificent finds from the Middle Ages is this gold clasp discovered in the Motala river at Kimstad in Östergötland. Set with sapphires, rubies and amethysts it was made in Paris in the 14th century. Could this have been brought into Sweden by Queen Blanche?

saints or other biblical figures. These could be authentic or avowed bone fragments, teeth, hair, or scraps of textile. Particularly sought after were nails or parts of the Holy Cross, or thorns from Christ's Crucifixion crown. These details were kept in silver reliquaries. The shape of the reliquary would indicate its contents. Thus a reliquary formed as a hand holding a pen is believed to have contained the finger bone of St. Bridget. The hand of blessing with extended fingers once contained a relic of Bishop Eskil, apostle of the province of Sörmland.

The largest collection of relics in Scandinavia was in Lund cathedral where they saved everything they could, from what was claimed to be a strand of St. Peter's beard to fragments of the Tree of Paradise.

The Church and the saints endowed us with new names, most of which are still in use. Anders, Lars, Bengt, Nils, Per, Mats and Johan came from the saints, while Andreas, Laurentius, Benediktus, Nicholaus, Petrus, Matias and Johannes are of biblical and papal origin. Girls were christened Maria, Elisabet (John the Baptist's mother), Margareta (saint) and Kerstin or Kajsa (after St. Catherine of Alexandria).

The nationalist revival which swept the country after the Battle of Brunkeberg engendered a renewed interest in Sweden's national culture. This led to the founding of Uppsala university in 1477; Scandinavia's first university. Here Ericus Olai wrote the first account of Sweden's history, in Latin: "Chronica Regni Gothorum" (A history of the Kingdom of the Goths). Prior to this Swedes who wished to study had to travel abroad. In Paris during the Middle Ages there were three established schools for Swedish students where over 900 Swedes and Finns pursued their studies. In the 15th century the German universities became the most popular in this respect.

The first book press in Sweden was set up by the Grey Friars at Riddarholmen in Stockholm in 1480. The printer was a German, Johan Snell, and his first book was a fable-type religious tract in Latin.

Paris was the centre of education and enlightenment and France altogether was a source of inspiration for Swedish art and ecclesiastical architecture. It was French architects who designed the cathedrals in Uppsala and Skara, and the Franciscan church at Riddarholmen in Stockholm. The exterior and interior sculptural embellishment of these churches was inspired by Paris.

Colour was paramount at this time. The exuberance of the Renaissance was reflected in warm, clear colours. Fashions were bold and resplendant in the attire of both lords and town burghers. The buildings were brick-red and in the churches there were vivid murals describing biblical events and scenes from the lives of the saints.

Even the music came from France and there are still traces of this influence in Sweden's folk dances and ring-games.

THE STOCKHOLM BLOODBATH, 1520

The first week of November 1520 must have been a frightening time for the citizens of Stockholm.

The struggle against the Danish king and the union had continued through the years following the Battle of Brunkeberg. But in 1520 Sweden's regent Sten Sture the Younger was killed. . . The new Danish king, Christian II, had been victorious and had now come to be crowned in Stockholm and to revive the union.

To begin with there was rejoicing and enthusiasm over the prospect of the coronation, but abruptly on the third day of the celebrations the lords and officials along with their wives were summoned to the royal palace. The festivities were over. Doors were closed and guards posted. The day of reckoning had come. Archbishop Gustav Trolle, the regent's principal enemy throughout the campaign against the Danes and the union, now demanded retribution and compensation for the destruction of his castle and the other indigities he had suffered. A specially appointed court quickly announced that offences against the archbishop amounted to heresy – and the heretics were to be executed.

All the relations and supporters of the Stures, enemies of the union, were arrested. A certain Bishop Hans Brask contrived to save his own skin however. Certainly he had been among those who had attacked the archbishop, but he had managed to conceal a little note worded: "To these things am I coerced and compelled" and this, bearing his seal, exonerated him.

The next morning, Thursday November 8, 1520, the guilty parties were executed in the main square of what is now Stockholm's Old town. The nobles were beheaded and the commoners hanged. Blood flowed through the alleyways. This terror continued for three days. Between 80 and 90 people were slain, their bodies left on the square. The church bells tolled around the clock while the stank of putrefying corpses poisoned the air.

Among those slaughtered victims were bishops, counsellors of the realm, supporters and relations of the Stures and many of Stockholm's leading citizens. The majority of the victims, however, were ordinary citizens.

A few days later Christian II announced a second feast, to be held in the city hall on the main square where blood still stained the cobblestones. This was a banquet and dance for the new counsellors of the realm to celebrate the birth of Christian II's daughter. At the same time Christian held a meeting with the mayor of Stockholm when he presented his plans for a new Scandinavia; a stronger union in which the three kingdoms would form a trading company that would defeat the Hanseatic League and collaborate with the Dutch.

When the news of the Stockholm bloodbath spread, those who

On the main square in Stockholm's Old Town on November 8, 1520, between 80 och 90 people were executed by order of Christian II of Denmark. Most of these were supporters or members of the Sture dynasty. In this way Christian hoped to destroy the opposition to Denmark and the union. He subsequently presented a plan for a new, more extensive union. But he was too late. The young Gustav Eriksson who had lost his father and other relatives in the bloodbath, fled to Dalarna where he began a rebellion which would enable Sweden to break away from the union and once more become independent.

were left of the Sture supporters fled for their lives in all directions. One of these was the 25-year old nobleman Gustav Eriksson who in the massacre had lost his father and many relatives while his mother and sisters had been taken to Copenhagen as prisoners. Gustav Eriksson fled northward towards Dalarna from where a few months later he was to lead an insurrection and scarcely two years afterwards would himself ride into Stockholm as the liberator of Sweden and the nation's new king, Gustavus Vasa.

Who, meanwhile, was really responsible for the Stockholm bloodbath? Archbishop Trolle? King Christian II? Someone else? The main burden of responsibility lay with Christian who could have stopped the slaughter. He, in fact, was probably encouraged by his Danish adviser Didrik Slagheck. Archbishop Trolle was used by Christian as an implement to attain his ultimate aim: the final and total destruction of the Stures. Yet in the end the Stockholm bloodbath was the decisive factor leading to the struggle which would dissolve the union forever; a struggle which had already begun.

Royal election, 1523

No one knows what really happened when the young Gustav Eriksson reached Dalarna after he had fled northward following the Stockholm bloodbath. His adventures at that time were never authentically documented, but the general gist of the many versions was widely spread even during his lifetime. Christian the Tyrant was fully aware, however, that the young Sture supporter, personally ambitious and with all the qualities of a good leader, had very quickly organized an armed insurrection in Dalarna. Gustav Eriksson was a member of one of the oldest and wealthiest land-owning families in Uppland. The Bergslagen people and the Dalecarlians were influenced at this time not only by the news of Christian the Tyrant's bloodbath and terror regime, but also by the rumours of new plans for the union which, if put into effect, would clearly be to the diadvantage of both the mining and foundry communities.

After a few successful local sorties the rebel force seized Västerås and the revolt spread through the Mälar valley and out across the country. At an early stage Gustav Eriksson gained the confidence of the Council of the Realm and the leaders of the Church, thereby securing additional support. People from all levels of the community joined him and in August 1521 in Vadstena he was proclaimed regent of Sweden. He was 25 years old.

Christian's troops still held Stockholm and the other principal towns.

Pursued by the king's troops Gustav Eriksson urged the people of Dalarna to follow him.

So Gustav Eriksson appealed to Lübeck which dispatched a fleet and a force of mercenaries. Stockholm was subsequently beleagured and forced to capitulate.

On June 6, 1523, the 27-year old Gustav Eriksson was elected king of Sweden and became Gustavus Vasa. This ceremony took place under somewhat unusual circumstances at a national assembly in Strängnäs.

Present were representatives of the domains of all the lawmen in Sweden and Finland, besides the envoys from Lübeck who entered on each side of the newly elected king and sat at his right hand during the church ceremony.

But the Dalecarlians were cautious and they hesitated despite Gustav Erisson's impassioned address at a meeting in Mora. He then set off on skis for Norway but the Dalecarlians changed their minds and came after him. They would support Gustav Eriksson and his cause.

Without Lübeck's mercenaries and money Gustav Eriksson could not have succeeded.

On June 24, he rode through the southern gateway of war-stricken Stockholm to take possession of the most important palace in the realm.

Never again would Stockholm be beleagured by an enemy.

But when he made this triumphal entry into the capital the Lübeckans rode close behind him. They were never to let him forget that he had acquired his crown on credit.

This war of liberation had cost 114 500 marks, a gigantic sum at that time.

In order to secure any credit at all Gustavus Vasa had been compelled to grant Lübeck and the Hanseatic League monopoly rights for all Swedish and Finnish foreign trade, besides numerous other significant privileges.

Sweden's finances were thus in a very poor state and the future prospects of the young king did not seem particularly bright. He was still not recognized by any foreign power. He had no proper army or fleet, no public officials and no diplomats and, what was worse, he himself had no experience of how a kingdom should be ruled and administered. In the south the Danes were still a serious threat and in the rural areas there was persistent unrest.

Nevertheless the union with Denmark had now been dissolved finally and absolutely and Sweden had become an independent state.

Thus we celebrate our National Day on June 6.

His crown may have been mortgaged and the throne still insecure, but the man who was to rule Sweden was confident that he knew what to do and he began at once. This was the advent of a new era.

Gustavus Vasa

This is how we have come to know Gustavus Vasa, a severe yet sound man, the saviour of the realm.

He had little or no political experience when at the age of 27 he became king. What he did know, however, was how to administer estates and farms and he thus treated the kingdom and his subjects as his private lands and employees.

The war debts to Lübeck were paid off with revenue "borrowed" from the Chuch. At the same time Gustavus Vasa was quick to recognize the advantages of Protestantism, the new doctrine from Germany. By making himself head of the Church he could ensure control of the bishops, the priests and their properties. Sweden thus became the first country in Europe to break with Rome.

And the outcome of all this was a cultural revolution.

Gustavus Vasa ordered the confiscation of the Church's printing presses and introduced the first censorship law. The reformer, Olaus Petri, was made responsible for the first Swedish version of the New Testament and not long afterwards the entire Bible. A few years later

Gustavus Vasa laid the foundations of modern Sweden. His methods were harsh and for his subjects he was no benevolent father of the people, but rather a ruler who attained respect through fear. He adopted Protestantism because he needed the Church's money and also because he was determined to deprive the bishops of their power.

the New Testament and parts of the Old Testament appeared in Finnish. The Swedish and Finnish bibles, printed in Stockholm, endowed the people in the two halves of the kingdom with their first common vocabulary, for Swedish and Finnish were now used in all the churches in all the provinces, irrespective of local dialects.

But at the same time this severed Sweden's centuries-old connections with the cultural centres of Europe for several generations to come. Uppsala university remained closed for almost a hundred years while schools and care of the sick and poor, traditionally administered by the Church, were neglected.

This was disastrous for education and training.

These convulsive reforms gave rise to numerous revolts, especially in Dalarna where the people who had initially been instrumental in bringing Gustavus Vasa to power felt themselves betrayed by their king. Småland proved the greatest threat here. Nils Dacke led the peasants' protests against taxes, Church reforms and ruthless bailiffs, when the entire province attempted a last revolt against the central powers. But all opposition was suppressed by a combination of negotiations, false promises, cold steel and fire, sometimes with the aid of the king's foreign mercenaries. Any opposition leader who failed to flee the country was executed.

The king had a hand in everything. He issued decrees on how the peasants should look after their bees and slaughter their sheep, bring in the hay and dig their ditches. The decrees, poured out of the royal chambers in an endless monologue to the people. Those who failed to act on His Majesty's authoritative advice incurred his immediate wrath. If a property was not run according to his requirements then he would take it over himself. He was tyrannical and unpredictable, but at the same time he was one of the few Swedish monarchs who had any concept of basic industry.

He ruled autocratically and established hereditary succession, but he also laid the foundations of modern administration and tax enforcement, centrally controlled from Stockholm. Throughout the realm redoubtable fortresses were built for military defence and administration, though also to make it quite clear who now exercised power over both Church and lords.

When Gustavus Vasa died Sweden was a united, centrally governed, independent nation with its own foreign policy, its own military defence and a substantial degree of self-subsistence.

Despite all the discord and harshness Gustavus Vasa's reign was a great success; for the country; for the people, and not least for the king himself. No Swedish monarch has ever left such a large personal fortune as Gustavus Vasa. He owned more than 5 000 freehold farms and more palaces and estates than anyone before or after. He was Sweden's biggest merchant, private banker, mine-owener, shipbuilder and shipowner.

Olaus Petri became one of the king's closest coadjutors, and one of his frankest critics. Like his master he exhorted the people to live lawfully and honestly; thundering forth his creed from the pulpit of Storkyrkan. *He became Sweden's best-known reformer, appointed by Gustavus Vasa to direct the translation into Swedish, first of the New Testament and then the entire Bible.*

The Vasa sons

Gustavus Vasa was a product of mediaeval culture, but his nine children – four sons and five daughters – were Renaissance individuals, as interested in the arts, as universally educated and as ruthless as any Renaissance prince in Europe.

The coronation of Erik XIV in Uppsala cathedral in 1560 was a spectacle of unprecedented splendour and it heralded the coming of another new era.

Even before Gustavus Vasa's death the struggle had begun between his sons; a contest which was just as bitter and brutal as any of the fraternal rivalries of the Middle Ages, though conducted in more elegant settings. Foreign masters had transformed the formidable strongholds of Gustavus Vasa into Renaissance palaces with elaborately decorated ceilings and panels, pavilions, formal gardens and fountains.

Erik XIV, who was both talented and artistic, conducted an active and forceful foreign policy. Estonia fell to Sweden and it was then that the dream was born of a future Swedish Baltic empire. This subsequently led to seven years of bloody war with Denmark, Lübeck and Poland. It was during this war that Sweden lost her only outpost to the west, Älvsborg, persecuted her provinces in the south and emptied the state coffers. During the ravages of these campaigns Erik XIV laid

Gustavus Vasa's sons were raised like Renaissance princes and they transformed the clumsy Vasa strongholds into handsome palaces in the style of the times. Erik XIV was extremely gifted and it was he who made the first move across the Baltic, seizing Estonia. Johan III was an introvert intellectual and mystic who dreamed of uniting the Protestant and Catholic faiths, but the youngest Vasa son, Charles XI, duly purged Sweden of the last traces of Catholicism.

waste large areas in Halland and burned all the farms on his way through Blekinge. In Ronneby 2000 people were massacred in a bloodbath which Erik later described elatedly as "a mighty slaughter where blood stained the waters of the river. . ." The Danes made equally brutal raids into Sweden, burning Jönköping and Vadstena and plundering Norrköping and other towns. It was these latter expeditions which engendered the Swedes' hatred of Denmark and for a long time made her the arch-enemy of Sweden.

Sweden retrieved vital Älvsborg through the Älvsborg Ransoms of 1570 and 1613. First she paid out 150 000 silver *daler* and then an even larger sum, 1 million *riksdaler*, which amounted to 25 000 kg of silver, an enormous amount of money at that time; the equivalent of 6 million barrels of grain.

One aspect of Erik's ambitious plans was to play court to the sovereigns of Europe, including England's Elizabeth I. He hoped to marry into European grand politics, yet in the end, to the disgust of his brothers, he married a gaoler's daughter, Karin Månsdotter, who became Queen of Sweden.

As time passed Erik became increasingly unbalanced and when he ordered the execution of three leading members of the Sture family his own brothers deposed him and committed him to prison. There he appears to have become totally insane and finally died, probably helped along by his brother Johan with whom he hade been involved in a lifelong feud.

Johan, an introvert intellectual and religious mystic, had against his brothers' wishes married a Polish Catholic princess, Katarina Jagellonica. Earlier, on account of his personal ambitions and political intriguing, Erik XIV had imprisoned Johan and his family in Gripsholm castle where Johan's son Sigismund was born. Sigismund inherited the Swedish throne, was elected king of Poland and, when the time was ripe, also became king of Sweden.

Sigismund then immediately entered into a feud with his uncle, Duke Karl, who had appointed himself Chancellor of the Realm and compelled the Swedish Church to make a final and total break with Rome. To be a Catholic was regarded as treason, the penalty for which was death.

In the propaganda of the time the struggle between Sigismund and Duke Karl was interpreted as a religious conflict. The final battle took place in 1598 at Stångebro outside Linköping. Duke Karl, who became Charles XI, was the victor. From then on Sweden was a totally Protestant state. This battle was followed by the Linköping bloodbath when Sigismund's followers were executed.

At this time Charles XI already had a son, christened Gustaf Adolf, whose future was predicted by the most eminent astrologer of the day, Tycho Brahe, on the island of Ven in the Öresund. He prophesied a brilliant royal career for the young prince.

Restructuring the community

There now followed a period of reconstruction never before witnessed in the country. In the course of some fifty years twenty new towns were founded in Sweden and ten in Finland and these were a great advance on the existing mediaeval, village-like communities. From now on every new town had its own defined plan, even though the results were perhaps not as impressive as the drawings.

All the buildings along a street should be in the same style while the streets themselves, at rightangles to each other, formed a chequered pattern. The ideas, the townplanners and the architects came from Holland, Germany and France. These masters could now design timbered buildings which were quite different from the traditional stone buildings of their own countries. Swedish towns were demolished and rebuilt. To achieve all this, however, rules, regulations and methods were needed - in other words, bureaucracy.

So Swedish bureaucracy is at least 300 years old and it was then that institutions such as the courts of appeal, the civil service departments, the Post Office and the Land Survey Board were created. Since the beginning of the 17th century Swedish civil servants have attended meetings, made their decisions, written their protocols and prescribed in detail how and where a building should be erected, where roads should be built and how people should live their lives.

The architect of much of this was the father of Swedish bureau-

Never was there such building activity as in the 17th century when more than 20 new towns were founded. Axel Oxenstierna laid the foundations for today's administration and bureaucracy systems in Sweden. The post office and parish registers were likewise established at this time and three new universities were founded, at Åbo, Lund and Dorpat.

This bronze bust of Gustavus Adolphus was sculptured by Hans von der Pütt in Nürnberg, 1632. It is one of the few portraits that the king himself sat for.

cracy, Axel Oxenstierna. He was Gustavus II Adolphus's Chancellor of the Realm and Sweden's first eminent statesman and administrator. And behind Oxenstierna was the one vital factor which necessitated the overall transformation of the community: war. Sweden was expanding rapidly around the Baltic and these campaigns demanded a growing supply of money and more and more soldiers.

This is why we have our parish records, among the oldest in the world. By referring to these the authorities could see where the recruits were to be found, for by this time the nucleus of Sweden 's army comprised conscripted peasants instead of expensive mercenaries.

Sweden was now divided into *län*, i.e. counties, each with its own governor. Competent civil servants and officers were needed for the new courts and civil service departments and for the army. Uppsala university was thus resurrected and expanded to encompass all the faculties. Three new universities were also founded: one at Lund, one at Dorpat in what was then Swedish Livonia and is today Tartu in Estonia, and one at Åbo (Turku). Of those universities which were founded beyond Sweden's present-day frontiers Åbo Academy still uses Swedish as its first language. The first *gymnasier*, high schools, were also opened now and a new national school system was introduced.

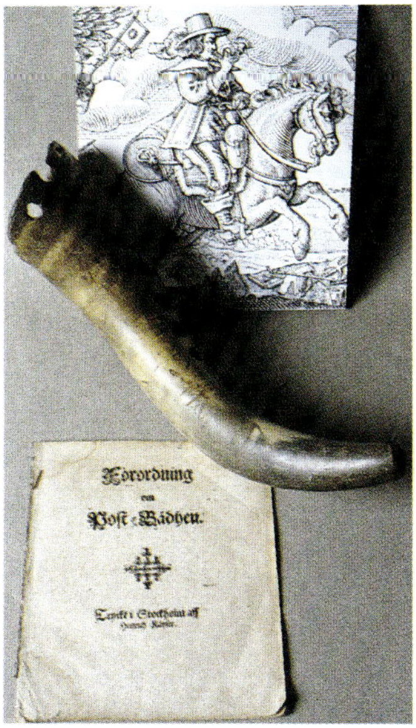

The postal service was established during the reign of Gustavus II Adolphus. Mail was delivered by post-runners and mounted postilions. The latter would sound his arrival by blowing his post horn. And, of course, they all had their printed instructions.

The most remarkable of all these new towns was Göteborg, planned entirely by Dutchmen who created here a miniature Amsterdam complete with canals. The first mayor of Göteborg was a Dutchman and Dutch was the language used in the city hall.

In addition, in order to ensure adequate communications between the capital and the provinces a postal service was organized. Delivery of a letter between Stockholm and Ystad should under no circumstances take more than five days and "post runners" who failed to maintain the required 10 km in two hours were liable to a week's confinement on bread and water!

Inns or posting-houses were established on the main highways where travellers could rest and change their horses. A day's journey was seldom more than 30 to 40 km along these rough roads.

The wars required a proper control over news services and the king had a reliable propaganda agency in the Church, since every citizen was bound by law to attend Sunday matins. From their pulpits the priests sternly pronounced to their congregations just what the king decided the common people should know. This was the public's only source of information until the first newspaper appeared in 1645: *Ordinari Post Tijdender*, issued by the Postmaster General in Stockholm. This paper became the official organ of every government. The name has changed at various times but it is still published daily: *Post- och Inrikes Tidningar*, now owned by the Swedish Academy.

The 30-years war

On June 26, 1630, Gustavus II Adolphus landed with his army on the island of Usedom off the coast of Pomerania. He at once knelt end prayed for victory in this great religious war which had already been waged on the continent for twelve years. It had begun when the Hapsburgian emperor Ferdinand sought to overrun the Protestant North German states and the situation was now critical.

At that moment the "Lion of the North" appeared on the scene to give renewed hope to the Protestants, according to the propaganda pamphlets which Gustavus had distributed. But the German Protestants were wary since they quite rightly surmised that Sweden's motives in this war were not altogether high-minded and selfless.

The Swedish losses were very heavy, half the army of some 15 000 young Swedes and Finns perished during the first three years and consequently reinforcements were constantly needed. The military successes, on the other hand, were considerable.

Gustavus II Adolphus is one of the few Swedes who enjoys any renown in international war history and this is mainly on account of the technical and strategic improvements that he contributed.

Every "honourable war" has its grim reverse side: the wounded, the dead, those who wait and hope in vain for a returning son or husband. Over 15 000 Swedish and Finnish youngsters perished in the 30-Years War. Gustavus II Adolphus himself was killed at Lützen on November 6, 1632.

Das Gebett

So Ihr Kön: May: in Schweden Anno 1630. im Monat Aprill in der Insel Riga ankommen/ da Er alßbald auff seine Knye nidergefallen/mit auffgereckten Händen zu Gott im Himel gethan.

ACh GOtt/ der du uber Himel und Erden/auch das wilde Meer herrschest/ wie soll ich dir gnugsamb dancken/ daß du mich dise gefährliche Raiß/ so gnädigklich beschützet hast/auch danck ich dir von äussersten meines Hertzens/und bitte wie du weist/daß diser mein Zug und Intent/ nicht zu mein/sondern einig und allein zu deinen Ehren/ und deiner armen und betrangten Kirchen zu Trost unnd Hilff angesehe/und geneigt: so wöllest mir auch/ so fern das Stündlein von dir bestimt/vorhanden/ darinnen du deinem Volck und Außerwöhlten Hülff senden wilt/ ferner Gnad unnd Segen/ auch sonderlich gut Wetter und Wind verleyhen und bescheren/daß ich mein hinderlassene Armada/ die ich auß mancherley Nationen versamblet/ mit frölichem Augen bald bey mir sehen/ und dein heilig Werck fortsetzen möge/ Amen. Und als seine Räth solch sein inbrünstig Gebett und Hertzbrennende Wort gehöret/ haben sie sich deß wainens nit enthalten können/ und als Er solches gesehen/ hat Er ihnen freundlich zugesprochen/ und gesagt/ mein wainet nur nicht/ sondern bettet fleissig/ je mehr bettens/ je mehr siegens/ hat darauff 200. Schiff mit Volck ans Land tretten lassen/ und die andern 200. anderstwohin Comandirt.

Zu Augspurg/ bey Hanß Jerg Mannasser/auffm Creutz.

On June 26, 1630, Gustavus II Adolphus landed on the island of Usedom off the coast of Pomerania, thereby involving Sweden in the great European conflict known as the 30-Years War. Sweden emerged from the final peace settlement as a major power with possessions in North Germany and along the Baltic coastline.

The Swedish army consisted of a motley collection of soldiers: Swedes and Finns and no less than 15 % mercenaries from Germany, France, England and Scotland.

They went from victory to victory. The triumph at Breitenfeld in September 1631 made Gustavus II Adolphus the greatest Protestant commander in the field and encouraged him to nurture increasingly ambitious plans for the future. It is probable that he envisaged himself as the Protestant emperor of an alliance between Sweden and the North German states.

The pinnacle of this success came in 1632 when he marched into Munich at the head of his army. Some months later for various strategic reasons the Swedish forces had to move northward and on November 6, 1632, they encountered the forces of the great Catholic general Wallenstein at Lützen.

This was one of the bloodiest battles of all for the Swedes. In the smoke and dust of the fighting the king rode by mistake into the enemy's lines, became involved in hand-to-hand combat and was killed. The Swedes managed to win the battle of Lützen nevertheless, though half their forces, 5 000 or more, were killed or wounded.

It took over a month for the news of the king's death to reach Stockholm.

Axel Oxenstierna did what he could to bring about an honourable withdrawal from this war. There was no peace, however, until 1648 and during that time Sweden attacked Denmark and in the final battles stormed and seized half of Prague. In the the peace settlement Sweden had acquired territories in North Germany and control over practically all the Baltic Sea rivers and important harbour towns. In the peace contract with Denmark a few years earlier she had secured Jämtland, Härjedalen, Gotland, Halland and the Baltic island of Ösel.

The late king's propaganda had proclaimed Sweden's glorious cause in defence of Protestantism and her own possessions on the Baltic. But each and every Swedish victory had incurred heavy losses and hardship both for the people back home and for those in the path of the triumphant army. The campaigning soldiers took whatever they wanted, plundering, burning farms and laying waste fields and crops. Women were violated and peasants whom the soldiers suspected of hiding gold or other treasures were tortured. The Swedes, said the Germans, were worse than either the Turks or the Tartars.

The victorious officers sent home valuable loot. They enjoyed promotion and honours while the common soldiers gained nothing. Those who were injured and invalided seldom received any help and afterwards became beggers and vagrants.

The rampages of the Swedes instilled such fear in the people that there are still ballads and rhymes in Poland, Germany and even south-eastern France, appealing to God to protect their children against the wild men from the North.

Falu mines, The armoury of Europe

The Falu mines were the heart of Sweden during the great power era. This era lasted just as long as the mines continued to function and Sweden remained the world's largest copper exporter.

But then the mines failed. That occurred around midsummer, 1687, by which time the mines were heavily overworked and there were only a few decades left of the great power era.

The Falu mines and the town of Falun became Sweden's first industrial centre where more than 5 000 people lived and worked. The ore was broken by fire. The miners dug their way into narrow tunnels by the light of tar torches and then built fires against the rock face so that it cracked and split. This was a heavy, hazardous job but Falu copper and iron provided 80% of Sweden's export revenue and supplied the iron for making cannon. Sweden was a leading manufacturer in this industry from that time right up until the present century.

Copper was also in great demand in the building trade throughout Europe. Baroque palaces and churches were roofed in copper and copper was used for making distillery equipment, pots and pans, and in the production of brass. The demand was unlimited, prices rose steeply and the Falu mines became a treasure trove for Sweden.

It was foreign capitalists and experts with new techniques and ideas who began the large-scale production of copper and iron in Falun and other places. The most eminent of these was the Dutchman Louis de Geer who became Sweden's richest man. He built up the export trade and secured a Swedish monopoly for the manufacture of cannon and muskets. He brought in a hundred or more Walloon families from the Netherlands, at that time the most skilled of craftsmen in forge work and iron production. They settled around de Geer's various ironworks at Finspång and other places, bringing with them their own clergy, schools and social systems. Most of the Walloons stayed in Sweden and became the forefathers of such well-known families as Allard, Wahl and Lamberts, Gauffin and Sporrong.

There were more foreigners than Swedes on the board of Sweden's first copper company, and likewise on the board of the tar-company. Specialists from Germany and Austria, among others Rademacher, de Besche and Geijer, improved the iron-producing methods and established new foundries and industries. The foreign specialists and financiers also remained in Sweden and many of them became nobles. More than half the families belonging to Sweden's House of Nobility are descended from these immigrants.

But even though it was these remarkably successful investors who headed the biggest concerns and were thus most prominent, it should nevertheless not be overlooked that the majority of the ironworks, etc. were in fact owned and run by Swedes.

The Falu copper mines were vital to Sweden as a great power, until they failed in 1687. During the 17th century more than 1 000 people were employed here, but they enjoyed none of the benefits of being citizens of a great power, their lot was one of atrociously heavy toil and constant danger. Ore and men alike were transported in big wooden tubs. The last load of ore was mined here in 1993.

An essential requirement for the proper functioning of this iron industry was, of course, sufficient manpower; miners under the ground and peasants in the vicinity to bring in timber for the mines and charcoal for the foundries. The Mälar valley peasants sold grain to the mining communities, from Hälsingland came butter and cheese, from Småland oxen and from Norrland salt fish.

The king wanted to raise the price of copper and make it as sought after as possible at home in Sweden. Thus the copper monetary unit was introduced. This was a pretty unwieldy currency, however, since a ten *daler* piece, or rather slab, weighed nearly 20 kg, so that anyone who wanted to pay in the largest "coins" needed a cart or sled to deliver them. The one advantage was perhaps that the sheer bulk of this money effectively deterred thieves. One can understand that people must have felt a considerable sense of relief when the Dutchman Palmstruch founded Sweden's first bank, *Stockholm Banco*, and issued Europe's first paper money. Shortly after this, in 1668, the National Bank of Sweden was established, *Riksens Ständers Bank*, the oldest surviving central bank in the world.

SWEDEN – A GREAT POWER

1650 was a year of triumph. Queen Christina, 23 years old had just been crowned to rule over a new major power in Europe. Christina was well educated and a good linguist. She sought to transform what she regarded as a somewhat rustic Swedish court into something more worthy of a great power.

Stockholm was rebuilt, as were several other mediaeval towns with their narrow, crooked alleys. Straight streets and blocks were introduced. In Stockholm the Norrmalm district was rebuilt to a plan which would survive until the 1960's, with Regeringsgatan named in recognition of Christina's regency and Drottninggatan after her queenship. In the Old Town, too, and on Riddarholmen fine houses were built which are still standing.

It was required, of course, that the sovereign of a major power in baroque Europe should be crowned in grandiose style and Uppsala was thus appropriately transformed. The city centre was demolished, fine straight streets were laid out and long approach roads built, all

Christina was 23 years old when she was crowned queen of Sweden. In her amibition to create a brilliant court around her she brought in eminent personalities from abroad and invested generously in art and culture. The spoils of war from Europe filled many of the big houses and shiploads of valuable books were donated to Uppsala university, including the 1400-year old "Codex argenteus".

The peace of Westphalia was signed in 1648 by which time the booty from war-ravaged Europe had been carried home to Sweden, including, for example, this magnificent gold crucifix.

Queen Christina's imposing arc de triomph *was erected and used once only, att her coronation. This drawing of the arch is from Erik Dahlbergh's "Suecia antiqua et hodierna".*

leading up to the cathedral and the castle. Then, to the dismay of the citizens of Uppsala, it was decided at the last moment that the coronation should take place in Stockholm.

The royal palace was fitted out with shiploads of furniture, tapestries and silver from the finest of Europe's workshops, besides much booty from the 30-years War: the emperor Rudolph's treasures from Prague with paintings by Rubens and Tizian, and priceless book collections including the Gothic 1400-years old *Codex argenteus* – now in the Uppsala University Library. Christina's private library became, in fact, one of the largest in Europe. The mansions of senior military officers were also rebuilt in classical baroque with interiors in the latest style. The most splendid of these was Skokloster, Field Marshal Carl Gustaf Wrangel's residence on Lake Mälar.

Never before or since have houses been built in Sweden to compare in magnificence with Wrangel's Skokloster, de la Gardie's Läckö and Oxenstierna's Tidö. All this can be studied in Erik Dahlbergh's imposing work "Suecia antiqua et hodierna", produced to show the world that Sweden, too, was well able to compete in wealth and splendour.

Most of these handsome buildings were designed by foreign architects and artists who afterwards settled here, for example Jean de la Vallé.

The first permanent foreign embassies were established at Christina's court and she brought in eminent scientists, artists, writers and musicians from many countries. One of the best known of these personalities was the French philosopher René Descartes.

It was Christina's intention to assemble a brilliant court around her and she therefore created more noble families than any other Swedish monarch. The House of Nobility was soon doubled numerically and these nobles became very powerful since the Crown in its constant need for money had been forced to mortgage more and more of its land to the nobility. Thus by now some 600 families had the right to levy taxes on two thirds of the homesteads in the realm.

Latin and French were used by the court and the sons of the nobles who studied abroad returned home as newly educated Europeans. Out in the provinces, meanwhile, many different languages were in use so that Sweden had become a multi-cultural and multi-lingual nation.

At the same time efforts were being made to create a national Swedish literature. In his writings George Stiernhielm, for example, sought to replace many of the foreign language terms and expressions by genuine Swedish and old Nordic words. There were even those who insisted that Sweden, the great power, should revive the runic script and form it into a pure Swedish alphabet.

Queen Christina abdicated in 1654, embraced the Catholic faith and settled in Rome where she was buried in St. Peter's Church. She was succeeded by her cousin who became Charles X Gustavus.

17th century Swedes showed a great interest in other parts of the world and in exotic materials. An example is this elaborately ornamented goblet in silver and rhinoceros horn.

Over the ice

The French ambassador, Terlon, had accompanied Charles X across the Danish ice and he reported home to Paris on this frightening expedition. During the first stage he rode with the king in a sleigh. When they approached the island of Fyn and made contact with the Danes the king and the ambassador left the sleigh and took to their horses. They then watched as the sleigh slowly sank through the ice and disappeared. Shortly afterwards two companies of German mercenaries and their horses went through a hole in the ice and perished.

Sometimes the course of history may be determined by sheer chance. The margin between total victory and absolute disaster can be very narrow, as tenuous as the ice when on January 30, 1658, in the middle of the night Charles X ordered his entire army to march acrosss the ice from Jutland to Zealand. The goal was Copenhagen.

For several days the might of Sweden was borne up by the shell of ice over Denmark's home waters.

This was a daring venture, one of the boldest in European war history. The troops began their march in darkness, their horses hauling the cannon across the creaking ice of the Little Belt and then via Fyn and successive islands, closer and closer to Copenhagen. At any moment this ice may have given way and the king and his best troops would have been lost in the bitter water. Or they might have found themselves stranded on an island; the easy victims of the enemy.

But this bold move was successful and the Swedish army grouped at Falster on February 11. The Danes duly surrendered and at the peace of Roskilde, February 26, 1658, Sweden regained the provinces of Scania, Halland, Blekinge and Bohuslän and also acquired the island of Bornholm and the province of Trondheim.

Charles X is said to have commented: "one must stake everything". He had done so and been triumphant, restoring Sweden's natural frontiers. But if the ice had not held that night then history might have been different. Perhaps Sweden would never have retrieved her southernmost province of Scania. She may even have been forced to surrender Öland and Gotland, Göteborg and possibly the entire province of Småland.

In the great flush of victory following this campaign Charles X dreamed of destroying Denmark altogether as an independent state and turning the Öresund into a Swedish-owned fairway. So he embarked on a new war, but now Holland and England entered the fray on Denmark's side. A Swedish attempt to storm Copenhagen failed and Denmark remained an independent kingdom.

Two years later, when only 37 years old, the fervently active Charles X Gustavus died suddenly of pneumonia.

War was the only thing that Charles X had really understood and he had hoped that through diverse regional wars of conquest he would be able to end the unrest in Sweden and also keep his large army busy and paid for. That is why he had attacked Poland without any tangible results, apart from the booty that his officers had seized. It was then that Denmark had declared war on Sweden and Charles X had immediately and hurriedly returned home, relieved to be pulling out of Poland with his honour intact.

Reorganizing the realm

And now the exhilaration was all over. Christina's pomp and splendour and Charles X's military ventures were done with and trite reality was at hand. The new king was Charles XI. He had no interest in foreign philosophers, he planned no spectacular festivities nor ran any risks.

Instead he produced results. The country became organized. Much of what we today term "typically Swedish" was formulated during the reign of Charles XI.

The nobles were forced to surrender much of what they had acquired during earlier regimes. The policy of reduction, i.e. restitution to the Crown, was carried through despite protest and clamour. Once a decision was made it was accepted, even among the richest and most powerful and this was something which had never before happened in Europe without rebellion by the nobles. Reduction was an alliance between the king and the people that had been begun during the reign of Charles IX and was now being revived. The Swedish peasants attained a status such as no other European peasantry enjoyed at that time. The Crown repossessed 30 % of the land.

The *indelningsverk*, or military-tenure system, was not Charles XI's innovation but he saw to it that the system was implemented and organized – so well that it survived until 1901. In this way Sweden could now keep a permanent army which would not require wars to sustain

The glory and the glamour ended with the accession of Charles XI. It was followed by a regime of restraint, discipline and order. It was now, too, that the witch hunts began in Sweden when more than 300 women were burned at the stake.

it. At the same time a naval base and shipyard was founded in Karlskrona.

The *indelningsverk* meant that a soldier was granted a smallholding and an annual wage for his livelihood. NCOs and officers – many of the latter were now commoners rather than nobles – were included in this system with smallholdings or farms according to their rank and dignity.

All this was patiently built up under Charles XI's tireless supervision. He could be up at two and three in the morning on his inspection tours. He might appear anywhere at any time; following military exercises or visiting government agencies to examine weapons, uniforms and accounts.

The new ecclesiastical statutes which to some extent remain applicable today, established the State Church. The parish clerks were responsible for teaching the children to read and write. All parishioners were required to attend church and were regularly interrogated on their knowledge and understanding of the Christian faith. From the pulpits the priests boomed forth the Christian ideals, emphasizing the congregations' duties to God, King and Country.

The Church was the king's voice throughout rural Sweden. The common people were kept "in the nurture and admonition of the Lord" and exhorted to abide by the Ten Commandments. In due course the Gustavus Vasa bible was replaced by the Charles XII bible.

Southern Sweden rapidly became Swedish again, even though the Danes encouraged guerilla tactics here, using marksmen as they called them, or *snapphanar* as they were known in Sweden. It was a combination of force and diplomacy that made this Swedification of the southern provinces possible. *Snapphanar* caught with weapons were brutally executed. At the same time psychological propaganda and indoctrination was used through civil servants at the newly founded university in Lund, and also through the parish priests who were now compelled to conduct their services in Swedish, and parish clerks who instructed children in the Swedish catechism.

Meanwhile this Lutheran doctrine and the warnings by the priests of the works of the devil led to a sudden witch hunt hysteria, something that had never arisen before during the Catholic era. Stories swept the country of witches' orgies with the devil on the Witches' Sabbath. It was alleged that they often took children with them and children's evidence was given particular credence. Over ten years as this hysteria spread across the country some 300 women were put to death, often after the most appalling torture. They were beheaded and then burned at the stake and it took a great deal of patience and persuasion by wise and enlightened individuals to put an end to this persecution.

Charles XII and the decline of a great power

About nine in the evening on Sunday November 30, 1718, Charles XII entered the trenches around the Halden fortress in Norway to inspect the work. For some weeks now the Swedes had been laying siege to this fortress and they were digging their way in closer and closer. It was a dark night, illuminated only here and there by the flashes of exploding shells. Suddenly the officers behind the king saw him collapse. He had been shot through the head and no one knows to this day where the bullet came from or who fired it.

But that fatal shot brought to an end Sweden's era as a great power.

For eighteen years Charles XII had defended the empire he had inherited. The Great Northern War had begun when Denmark, Poland and Russia attacked Sweden. The king, then only 17 years old, had immediately gone out into the field. The Carolean military-tenure system had functioned well; within a few months the entire army was mobilized, Denmark was beaten and after a series of brilliant campaigns Charles XII defeated first the Russians at Narva and then the Poles.

But then came reverses. Charles XII made a bold strike into the heart of Russia towards Moscow. This campaign failed, however, and the king and his army were forced to retreat into the Ukraine where they endured a winter of great hardship. It was there in the Ukraine that the Swedes encountered Peter the Great's forces at Poltava in 1709 and suffered a devastating defeat. The wounded king and a thousand or more of his army fled southward into Turkish territory.

Altogether some 30 000 of Charles XII's army, Swedes and mercenaries, ended up in Russia as prisoners-of-war. Among these were several thousand civilians since many of the officers took their families with them on their campaigns: women and children, servants, army chaplains and civil servants. These prisoners were transported to various parts of Russia. Many of them were used as forced labour to build St. Petersburg on captured Swedish territory, while others were moved out to Siberia.

The plague returned in the 18th century and, just as during the mediaeval Black Death, it was principally the rat which carried this dreaded infection.

Many of them died in Russia. Only about one fourth of the common soldiers and perhaps half the officers came home again after anything from five to thirtyfive years in captivity. In the meantime wives and children ran the smallholdings, farms and estates. Thousands of letters and diary pages describe the hardships of the prisoners-of-war and the endurance and loyalty of their families. These were years of crop failure, famine and disease in Sweden.

The majority of the well-organized Swedish prisoners maintained their nationality, language and religion throughout captivity and only a few entered the service of the Tsar. The Carolean discipline was proof against all their trials and hardship.

For several years from his base in Bender, Charles XII strove unsuccessfully to bring the Turks into the fight against Russia, but when he returned home the coalition war against Sweden continued, reinforced now by England and Prussia. Southern Sweden was seriously threatened and it was in this situation that Charles XII embarked on his last campaign in an attempt to strike against Danish Norway. His idea was that Norway should be integrated with Sweden and the Norwegians become Swedes. The only way to achieve this, he reasoned, was for his army to have its own stores and supplies there and to treat the Norwegians as allies rather than enemies.

In the state of uncertainty following the king's death at Halden a Russian galley fleet attacked up and down Sweden's east coast. Towns, foundries and a thousand or more farms were burned and more than 10 000 people were made homeless. Grain and livestock were carried off, but a Russian strike on Stockholm was halted and re pulsed well outside the capital.

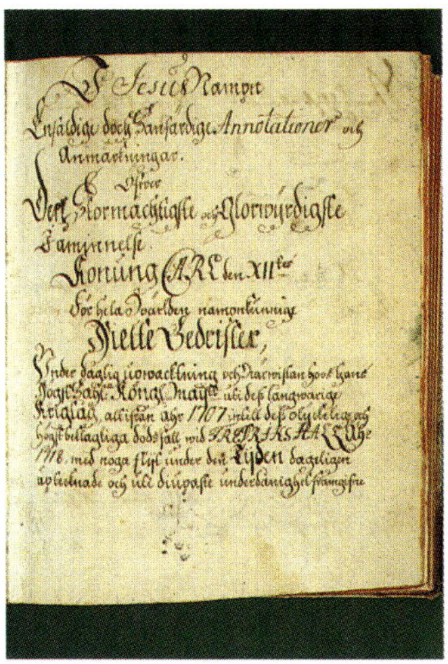

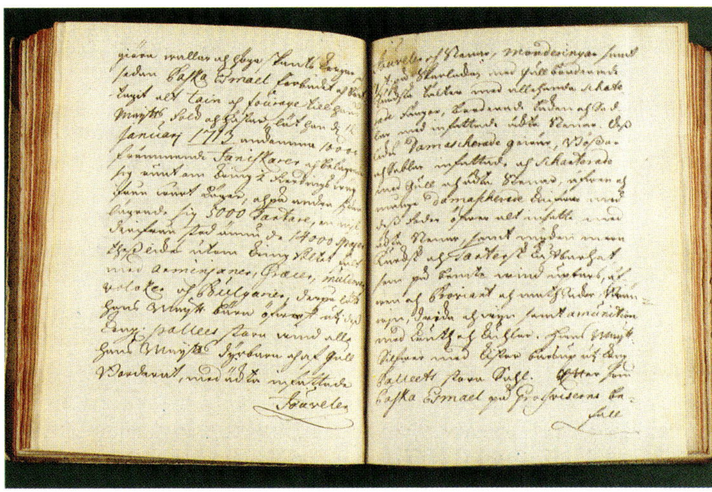

Johan Hultman did household service for Charles XII from 1707 until the king's death in 1718. He was constantly at the king's side, at Poltava, at Bender and in Norway. He left an account of his experiences during these years in his personal diary (above).

It is thanks to extant diaries that we also know how the Swedish prisoners-of-war survived in diverse parts of the vast Russian empire.

During the peace following 20 years of war Sweden was forced to surrender her Baltic provinces, parts of eastern Finland and most of her German provinces. This ended Sweden's era as a great power. All she had left was a handfull of small possessions in northern Germany.

The four estates

The bullet at Halden put an end to absolutism in Sweden. The power was now in the hands of the *Riksdag*. In fact, in due course King Frederick I did not even have to be present at the *Riksdag* assemblies, instead the Council, furnished with the king's signature-stamp could handle the proceedings.

It occurred later in history that for four short periods the authority of the *Riksdag* was restricted, but never again would a Swedish king rule autocratically.

This period is known in Swedish history as the Age of Liberty.

Even though this state of affairs was far from being democratic in the modern sense, more and more people were nevertheless having a say in what was happening. It was at this time that Sweden's first professional politicians emerged.

From the Middle Ages well on into the 19th century the *Riksdag* was made up of four groups, or Estates as they were known. Each of these Estates held its own assemblies at its own premises under the direction of its own speakers.

First and foremost came the nobles. The nobles, who amounted to no more than 0.5 % of the population, could produce as many as a thousand members at the House of Nobility assemblies, since the head of each and every family had the right to attend. Initially the nobles were led by Arvid Horn who became President of the Council, which made him more or less the equivalent of prime minister. It was he who actually ruled the country.

The clergy represented about 1 % of the population and this Estate was made up of all the bishops and an elected priest from each diocese, altogether about 50 members.

The burghers constituted 2 % of the population with an Estate of some 90 members, from every town in Sweden and Finland.

The great majority of the population, more than 90 %, were represented by 150 members of the peasants' Estate. But only peasant proprietors, i.e. freeholders, were eligible and entitled to vote. There was one such representative for every *härad*, i.e. township or jurisdictional district.

Now under its leader Olof Håkansson, the peasants' Estate which had existed since the early Middle Ages, became unique in Europe and the influence of the peasants gradually increased.

But a large part of the population continued to exist without any form of representation, namely the peasants who lived and worked on the nobles' estates, and all the cottars, crofters, tenement soldiers and paupers. Another large group without representation was made up of the commoner physicians, army officers and certain categories of civil servants.

The complex political intrigues between the different parties and among the Riksdag *committees created our first professional politicians. Olof Håkansson, for example, was appointed to the* Riksdag *in 1738. But woe betide that peasant who used "powder, carriage or chaise". For him there could be no career in the* Riksdag.

Absolutism was replaced by power in the hands of the Riksdag's Four Estates. To all intents and purposes the country was governed by the nobles' leader, President of the Council Arvid Horn. Not even the king's presence was needed, it was sufficient with his signature-stamp.

Adolph Frederick was Sweden's second monarch whose royal signature was substituted for a signature-stamp.

The most important work in the *Riksdag* was done by the committees, especially the *secret committees* which handled finance, defence and foreign policy. To begin with, however, no peasant had right of access to these committees since most of the peasant Estate representatives could perhaps read but certainly not write and were thus considered not qualified to take part in such elevated matters.

The *Riksdag* became an ungainly vehicle to steer. A great deal depended upon cooperation between the Estates' speakers. Very soon Sweden's first political parties emerged, known as the Hats and the Caps. These parties mainly embraced the first three Estates. They had their own programmes, clubs and activists or whips.

The Hats wished to promote industry and dreamed of collaborating with France to take revenge on Russia. They claimed that Arvid Horn's cautious policy was conducted in his nightcap and they were thus dubbed the Hats, and their opponents the Caps. The Caps favoured agriculture and sought the support of England who was Sweden's principal trading partner.

And just as many of the major powers behave today in the developing countries, so the English, French and Russian embassies bribed their sympathizers in the Swedish *Riksdag*. Corruption was widespread and occurred within all four Estates.

The Dalecarlian insurrection

Revolution threatened Stockholm in 1743. Several thousand armed peasants marched into the capital to protest against war, high prices and a proposed German prince as heir to the Swedish crown. The revolt was ruthlessly crushed and this was the last time ever that a province attempted to rebel against the central powers in Stockholm.

On June 22, 1743, Stockholm was on the brink of revolution. An armed mob came face to face with the army at Gustaf Adolfs torg in the heart of the capital. The government was paralyzed, the king powerless and the people seething with anger. This was known as the *Great Dalarna Dance* and it ended in blood and tears. The background was as follows. The revengist Hats who held the power saw their chance in 1741 and declared war on Russia. This campaign was poorly planned and turned into an absolute disaster for the Swedish army. Of the 18 000 men who were deployed in eastern Finland barely 7 000 returned. Most of them perished from disease and hardship and hundreds died on the way back.

In the subsequent peace negotiations Russia demanded that the sovereign bishop of Lübeck, Adolph-Frederick of Holstein-Gottarp, should be made heir to the Swedish throne. He was related to the Russian empress Elizabeth.

Crop failures, high prices, epidemics and unsuccessful war, an unknown German prince who was to succeed the extremely unpopular Frederick I – the latter had no legitimate offspring – all this fostered

discontent across Sweden, especially in Dalarna where the people had been severely stricken by the economic crisis and had protested from the outset against the war.

The Dalarna regiment had mutinied when they were about to embark for Finland; the soldiers refusing to go onboard unless the king himself went with them.

The people of Dalarna, like the entire peasant Estate, did not want Adolph-Frederick as crown prince, they demanded instead a Danish prince. Many of them had visions of a Nordic union, especially the Dalecarlians who had close economic and personal ties with Norway.

In May 1743 when the war was still not yet over, a proclamation of rebellion was issued from Mora. Falun was occupied and a force of 4 500 men set out for Stockholm, armed with maces, scythes and muskets. They took with them as hostages the governor of the province and other officials.

On June 20 they reached Norrtull in Stockholm where they were met by Frederick I who sought to reason with them. But they would not listen to "the old German" as they called him and when the king's troops refused to fire on the Dalecarlians the latter marched on into the heart of the capital.

Stockholm was seething by now, for a considerable part of the people sympathized with the men from Dalarna. The more unpopular politicians fled out into the country. What would happen next?

Then the news arrived from Finland that a preliminary peace had been reached with Russia and the Russians had repeated their demand: agree to Adolph-Frederick as heir to the throne and Sweden would be granted a more favourable peace.

This caused some confusion among the Dalecarlians who lacked any sort of plan for their next move. At about the samed time twelve ships entered Stockholm harbour carrying government troops and the government itself, hitherto paralyzed, now acted. The Dalecarlians were ordered to leave Stockholm immediately, but they remained and the cavalry moved in, surrounded the ill-armed force and cut it down. 140 died, many were wounded and the rest fled, pursued by the cavalry. Some managed to get back to Dalarna but over 3 000 were seized and locked up. Six of the leaders were beheaded while many others were flogged and then imprisoned for life, as were the king's soldiers who had refused to fire on them.

Thus the sovereign bishop of Lübeck, Adolph-Frederick of Holstein-Gottorp, was able to enter his new kingdom. He turned out to be a reasonable if insignificant fellow who is said to have been happiest squatting at his turning-lathe, pipe in mouth.

So the last ever popular rebellion in Sweden was quashed. Never again would a province attempt an armed revolt against the central powers in Stockholm and this also terminated the final remnants of independence among the provinces.

New times, new ideas

Carl von Linné was Sweden's first scientist of international repute. Linné was representative of modern Sweden and of much of what we regard today as typically Swedish. One should not be deceived by his 18th century powdered wigs and silken coats for here was a man who thought as we think nowadays, who hummed some of the same airs and was possibly surrounded by the same furniture as we have in our homes today.

The transition from great power to the Age of Liberty was almost as much of an upheaval as had been the Reformation two hundred years earlier. What took place in Sweden over a period of fifty years was unparalleled in the country's history. This was the time of enlightenment, innovation and reason. The new ideas came originally from England and were transmitted across Europe by French intellectuals.

In Sweden the burgher class, that is to say the middle class, emerged. The prevailing concepts were practical, optimistic and reformist. The natural sciences were in the ascendancy. The universe, nature and mankind functioned according to established laws. Existence in its entirety could be comprehended, provide one exercised common sense and curiosity.

In this exhibition we see Linné amidst a collection typical of the times, objects selected från different parts of Sweden and many other countries.

Mankind was now to be freed from every form of prejudice and oppression. In mid-18th century Sweden there were the same high standards of science as in France and England. Swedish botanists such as Linné, physicists like Celsius, astronomers and statisticians like Wargentin and many others, enjoyed universal renown. The mathematician, inventor and visionary Emanuel Swedenborg was in a category of his own. Natural science should be a practical and useful of learning pursued for the benefit of all.

That is why the Royal Academy of Sciences was founded, not only for the purpose of the natural sciences as such, but also as a medium for the development and improvement of trade, technology and industry.

In this spirit many inventions appeared which can still be found in the Swedish home, for example the tile stove. The government invested in domestic industries and very soon more than 14 000 people were employed in newly opened textile mills.

Linné travelled to Lapland and other Swedish provinces, writing books on his observations which still make interesting reading today. New regions were opened up and young people were encouraged by tax reliefs to leave the Norrland coastal areas and move inland to Lapland. Here they would break new ground and farm new land in places where previously there had been no permanent settlements. This led in

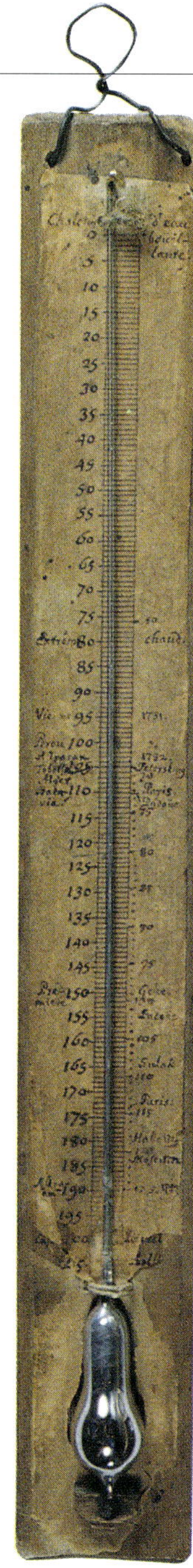

Celsius's first thermometer had a reversed scale where freezing point was registered at 100° and boiling point at 0°.

its turn to disputes with the native Lapps over fishing waters and grazing pasture. But the cultivation and settlement of new areas had now definitely begun.

To get Sweden moving with her new factories and agricultural projects more people were needed, so larger families were encouraged and a special population census commission was appointed. In time this became the Central Bureau of Statistics, the first institution of its kind in the world.

All these new ideas, dreams and plans were documented and discussed in a variety of new publications, for there was now freedom of the press in Sweden. The first writer to gain general popularity was Olof Dalin with his journal "The Swedish Argus". Art and literature flourished as never before. The Swedish Academy was founded in 1786, and artists and writers were granted royal stipends. We still sing Bellman's songs and admire Sergel's sculptural works and Tessin's handsome buildings, palaces and manorhouses in the rococo style, while skilled craftsmen produced fine furniture that is still much sought after at the quality auctions. Stockholm's opera house was built and the Royal Dramatic Theatre was founded.

Art, fashions and interior decorating styles were brought in from France. Sweden developed her own version of French rococo, the Gustavian style, which has never become outdated nor lost its appeal in the Swedish home.

The first person in Sweden to produce distilled liquor from potatoes was Eva Ekeblad (1724–86). She also became the first woman member of the Royal Academy of Sciences. Right: a wax doll of Carl von Linné from Madame Tussaud's in London. The Moroccan lion belonged to Gustavus III and was kept in the lion's den where the Nordic Museum now stands. It was shot in 1792 after the king had been assassinated. Below: contemporary illustrations for medical science were often of a somewhat bizarre or frightening nature.

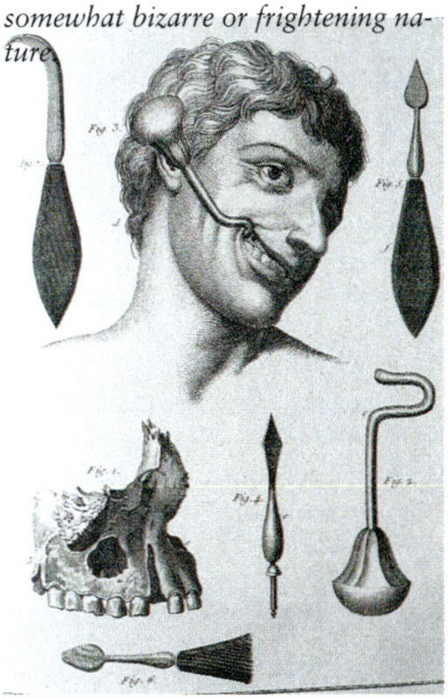

Revolution

In France it was primarily the frustrated middle classes who beheaded their king, abolished the nobility and prepared the way for a new society under the battlecry Liberty, Equality, Fraternity.

In Sweden it was the king himself who implemented the revolution, did away with rights and privileges and fostered the middle classes. And he achieved this without spilling a drop of blood and before the Parisians had stormed the Bastille. The king was Gustavus III.

When Gustavus learned that he was to become king of Sweden he was attending the opera in Paris and, ironically enough, he was to die at the opera – in Stockholm. His entire life as monarch was a drama in which he himself played the leading role.

During Adolphus Frederick's reign the sovereign had lost his status. The *Riksdag* was paralyzed by party conflicts and by the struggles between the nobles and the commoners.

On August 19, 1772, Gustavus III staged a *coup d'état*. The counsellors of the realm were locked in the palace and secret committees were abolished for ever. Very quickly the king's supporters seized control and a few days later the Estates were summoned to the Throne Room. They were confronted with loaded cannon as they approached the palace. The king now declared that since he could no longer tolerate "the insufferable aristocratic despotism" there was to be a new constitution.

As from now the king had more to say in all matters, the nobles were deprived of their power and the middle classes were in the ascendancy.

Gustavus III has been called "the theatre king", but he was also a very able and resolute politician who swiftly and effectively destroyed the power of the Swedish nobility. The Union and Security Act of 1772 determined what was to happen henceforth.

The dainty, ethereal 18th century dining room became a symbol of Scandinavia and the northern light. It founded the concept of the ideal home interior as developed i.a. by Ellen Key and Carl Larsson, where simplicity was the essential feature.

Various popular reforms were announced. Trading in grain was allowed by everyone. The death sentence for witchcraft and sorcery was abolished. Torture was forbidden and religious freedom was proclaimed, thus Catholics were allowed to hold their own services and Jews were permitted to settle in Sweden. Less popular, meanwhile, was the decision to introduce a State liquor monopoly!

Gustavus III calculated he would be able to restore the support of the nobles if he could conduct a successful war, and when Russia became involved in a war with Turkey he decided the time was ripe and that, among other things, he would attack St. Petersburg. This campaign was a total disaster, however. Part of the officer corps rebelled in Finland and the king's position appeared critical. When the news then came that Denmark had declared war on Sweden, Gustavus returned at once to Stockholm and, like Gustavus Vasa, made his way up to Dalarna where he addressed the people of Mora and exhorted them to set up a force of volunteers for the defence of the realm. A contingent of recruits from the Siljan valley duly arrived in the capital and some of these were quartered in Drottningholm palace where the king again addressed them personally.

Gustavus III's audacious policy earned him many enemies. Anckarström, who actually shot the king, was merely the tool of a very large conspiracy organized by the nobles.

The war against Denmark served as a sort of diversion and the king returned to Stockholm where with the aid of the commoner Estates he abolished once and for all most of the privileges of the nobles. He forced them to accept his reforms by himself assuming the chairmanship of the House of Nobility.

The commoners were now given right of access to most of the government offices and the peasants were granted full rights of ownership to their land, in other words they were permitted to hunt and fish there, which hitherto had been the privilege only of the nobles. Elsewhere, meanwhile, there was less enthusiasm, for the king had reintroduced absolutism and abolished the 500-year old Council of the Realm. Nevertheless in time Gustavus's reforms would lead to an almost total transformation of the community, because it was now that the political and social advance of the lower classes actually began.

Of course the king had acquired many enemies, especially among the nobles who regarded him as a tyrant. On March 16, 1792, the underground opposition struck. An officer and nobleman, Jacob Johan Anckarström, shot Gustavus III at a masked ball in the opera house. The king was carried bleeding to the palace where he died thirteen days later.

The assassin was seized the day after the deed, identified by the pistol he had discarded after the shooting. Several of his fellow conspirators were sentenced for murder but only Anckarström was executed. For three days he was flogged at various public places in Stockholm before he was beheaded near Skanstull on the outskirts of the city. This was the last time that a political offender was executed in Sweden.

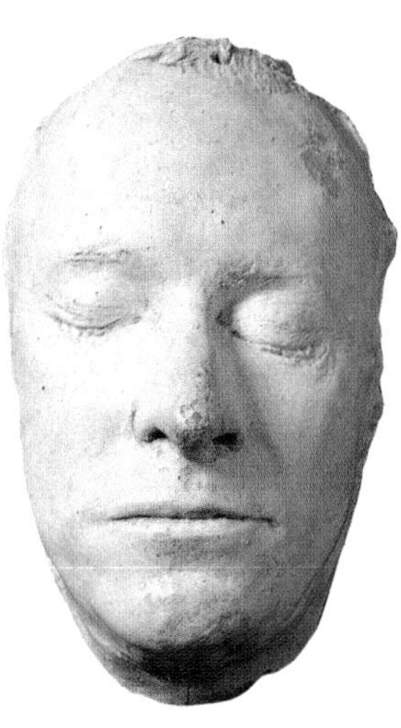

Death-mask of Gustavus III.

The loss of Finland

Gustavus III was succeeded by his son Gustavus IV Adolphus and it was then that the brilliant Gustavian era came to an end with one of the greatest disasters in Swedish history.

Sweden lost Finland and thereby one third of her total area and one fourth of her population. For over 700 years Finland had been just as much a part of Sweden as the province of Scania, though for twice as long.

All at once Stockholm, which had hitherto been securely located in the middle of the realm, became a sort of frontier city with the Cossacks not far off to the east. All this came as a severe political, economic and psychological shock to Sweden at that time.

The drama had begun in January 1808. Napoleon's armies were advancing across Europe. Russia and France had formed a secret alliance that should compel Sweden to join the war against England. But Gustavus IV refused. He was one of the few monarchs who dared gainsay Napoleon.

So Russia attacked Sweden. More than 20 000 troops crossed the frontier into Swedish Finland while at the same time, under the command of Marshal Bernadotte, French troops reached Denmark ready to attack Sweden from the south.

On orders from Stocholm the Swedish-Finnish army then withdrew northward towards Österbotten to await reinforcements, while the newly-built Sveaborg fortress at the approaches to Helsinki would, it was reckoned, contain the Russian troops in southern Finland. Thus far everything went according to plan.

But Sveaborg was surrounded and cut off. The Russians employed a skilful form of psychological warfare which quickly convinced the commander of the fortress, Carl Olof Cronstedt, that the position was hopeless and he capitulated. More than 7 000 soldiers, 110 ships, 2 000 cannon and ammunition and supplies now fell into Russian hands.

This dishonourable loss of Sveaborg was a hard blow for Sweden and the Russians continued to keep the initiative in the war. All this is dramatically described in Johan Ludvig Runeberg's "Lieutenant Stål's Legends" and characters here like Sven Duva, Adlercreutz, von Döbeln and Lotta Svärd existed in reality. Then in March 1809, at the height of the war, Gustavus IV Adolphus was deposed in Sweden's one and only military coup. He was seized in his bedchamber by six officers. He signed his abdication and after a few months internment at Gripsholm castle he and his family left the country. He subsequently called himself Colonel Gustafsson, lived a somewhat itinerant, lonely life and died at an inn in Switzerland in 1837.

The war with Russia could have ended even more disastrously,

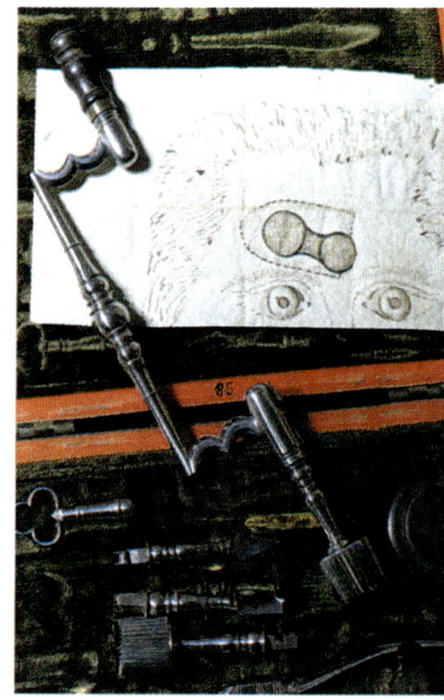

In 1791 General von Döbeln was struck in the head by a musket shot and the physicians had to drill a hole in his skull. Now once again the hero of many Finnish battles exhibited his extraordinary courage and endurance. By means of a mirror he watched the entire operation and made his own sketches of how it was performed.

It is difficult for us today to appreciate just how shocked Sweden must have been at the loss of Finland, which for 700 years had been an integral part of the realm. All at once Sweden had lost one third of her territory and one fourth of her population. Stockholm, which had hitherto been in the middle of the kingdom, had now become a frontier post to the east.

since the Russian troops had penetrated northern Sweden and occupied among other places the coastal town of Umeå, Russia wanted to make the Kalix river the frontier line, in which case the whole of what is today Finnish-speaking Norrbotten would have become part of Finland. At the same time farther south the Cossacks crossed the ice from the Åland islands and seized the little town of Grisslehamn. This caused great trepidation in Stockholm, but the Russians returned to Åland the following day. In the peace negotiations Sweden manged to secure the Swedish-Finnish frontier as it is today. By this time Finland had already become a Russian Grand Duchy, while retaining her own laws. On account of this the 1734 Swedish laws survived in Finland right up until our day and it is also because of this that Finland has remained a bilingual nation.

In Sweden Gustavus III's brother became the next king, Charles XIII, and since he lacked heirs a Danish prince was elected successor to the throne. But the prince died suddenly and at his funeral Axel von Fersen, the last of the great Gustavian leaders was beaten to death by a mob while the troops failed to intervene. Afterwards the French marshal, Jean Baptiste Bernadotte was elected successor to the Swedish throne and in 1818 he became King Charles XIV John.

Peace, vaccine and potatoes

Now for the first time the Swedish people were about to enjoy the benefits of protracted peace. From the year 1814 when the Swedish-Norwegian union was formed Sweden entered upon the longest unbroken period of peace of any country in European history.

The loss of Finland had been a severe psychological shock which was to influence national policy and culture for decades to come. But at the same time it engendered a new spirit of determination. Finland should be retrieved, patriotism flourished and many sought inspiration from far back in their history; in the strength of the Goths and the Aesir gods.

The entire country was transformed and even the landscape changed as people's lives changed. New ideas emerged, some brought in from abroad, others evolved at home. Despite the stubborn opposition of the more conservative farmers, new techniques were introduced using modern ploughs and harrows. New crops were raised on larger fields. Ditches were dug, trees felled, the water level of lakes was lowered and rivers were cleared and diverted so that floating timber could bypass waterfalls and rapids.

Land parcelling was enforced, in 1807, in 1813 and in 1827. In this way the old villages where the families subsided on their small strips of land here, there and everywhere, were reorganized so that each family would have the largest possible plot or plots to work.

The Värmland farmer Gustaf Persson, like many others, now began to recognize the value of the potato which had hitherto been grown mainly as an ornamental plant. Potatoes were a more worthwhile crop than turnips – not to mention that one could make *brännvin*, i.e. aquavit, out of them.

It was at this time, too, that one of Charles XII's discoveries in Turkey was introduced in Sweden: innoculation with a smallpox vaccine. Then around the turn of the century they began to use cowpox vaccine with its less virulent side effects. This method came to be known as vaccination (Latin *vacca* = cow) and by 1804 vaccination was being used throughout the country.

When Beata Nilsdotter gave birth to her child the midwife could use delivery intruments and with safer deliveries and vaccination against smallpox and the like, more and more infants survived their first year of life.

Thus peace, vaccine and potatoes, as the author Tegnér wrote, explained the sharp rise in population which was now occurring.

Never before in Sweden had there been such investments in communication facilities. New roads and canals were built, the latter including the Trollhätte canal, the Södertälje canal and, largest of them all, the Göta canal right across the country. Over 6 000 soldiers took

Per Lindroo's panorama of 19th century Swedish farming and forestry work is based on the detailed diary of the Värmland farmer Gustaf Persson. Persson describes the manifold activities of the farmer's year, including work at the charcoal stack, at the watermill and at the little sawmill. Lindroo's presentation illustrates the changes in the Swedish landscape caused by modernization and progress. This exhibition also shows potato cultivation and visitors can see for themselves how the potato plants develop from day to day.

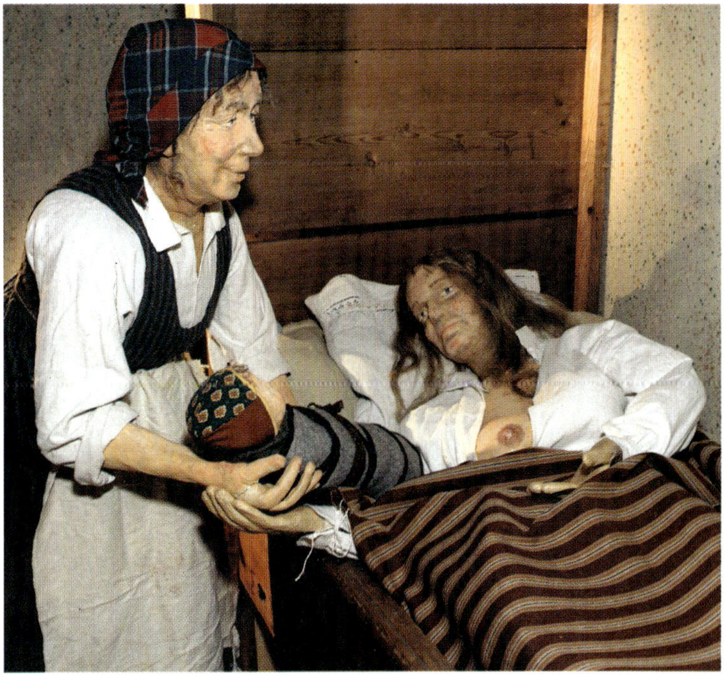

Gradually hygiene improved, as did medical and nursing techniques and procedures and the progress here is reflected in childbirth statistics. With new aids and methods the midwife could relieve the hazards and suffering of birth so that increasing numbers of newborn children survived.

part in the initial work on the Göta canal and by the time it was completed in 1832, 60 000 men had toiled for a total of 7 million workdays.

Tall chimneys could now be seen rising above the treetops. The Canal Company had set up a workshop in Motala and this developed into Sweden's largest modern industrial plant for building steam engines, steamboats, water turbines, bridge sections and, something totally new: locomotives.

The railways

The Stockholm-Uppsala railway was opened in 1866 and passengers travelled free of charge. But even as late as 1860 a domestic permit, or pass, was required to move around in Sweden, whatever one's means of travel.

The coming of the railway was something never to be forgotten among the local inhabitants. The opening of the local railway station was the event of the century. Sometimes the king was present, the province governor was most certainly there, and practically every person in the entire district of course. Regimental bands played and patriotic speeches were delivered as the train drew in, blowing steam and smoke and whistling in triumph. Vast quantities of food and drink were consumed at such ceremonies and, as the Lord Chamberlain noted indignantly at the inauguration of the Göteborg station: "The people ate pineapple like turnips and truffles like potatoes!"

The day the first locomotive came puffing through the forests heralded a new era. With much snorting and huffing the newcomer reached the unheard of speed of ten kilometers an hour. The incredible thing was, meanwhile, that the train could continue hour after hour without a pause; no change of horses, no resting time and often traversing countryside where there was not a road in sight.

Sweden's first railway was opened in 1856, a privately-owned line.

Meanwhile work had begun on the first State-owned lines, Stockholm–Göteborg and Stockholm–Malmö. In charge of this project was one Nils Ericsson, brother of John Ericsson who emigrated to the USA where he became a universally renowned inventor and designed among other things the marine propeller and the Monitor warship. Nils Ericsson became a canal builder in Sweden and was also known as "the father of the Swedish railway".

Nils Ericsson laid his tracks around the outskirts of the old towns and through neglected regions where new towns subsequently sprung up: Katrineholm, Hallsberg, Nässjö, Hässleholm and others. The main line westward to Göteborg was opened in 1862 when Charles XV rode through the countryside in an open railway coach, halting to speak to the local people at every station.

The railway lines northward took more time to build. The main lines to Vännäs and Boden were opened in 1891 and 1894 respectively and the one across to Jämtland in 1882. At the same time private companies began building their own lines, thereby gradually creating a new communication network throughout the country

Railways were laid to new industrial areas, while new industries grew up along the railway routes. Raw materials, finished products and people were transported twice as far, twice as quickly and at half the cost of the stage coaches. And during the years of famine in the 1860's aid and supplies could be carried by rail.

With the coming of the railways people, goods and even livestock could be moved around as never before. An entire region could be transformed, a community moved bodily and fuel and energy delivered wherever it was needed.

Trains were supposed to run on time. But whose time? Up until 1879 each region had its own local time. Thus there was a 24-minute difference between Stockholm and Göteborg.

After involved discussions the *Riksdag* finally agreed that a standard time should be established across the country, based on the meridian roughly half way between Stockholm and Göteborg. On January 1, 1879, all the clocks throughout the country were re-set and Sweden thus became the first country in the world to introduce standard time.

The railways turned Sweden into a north/south kingdom. Ever since the Middle Ages it had been a broad east/west realm with Stockholm, the capital, in the middle. The most important communications had run east/west from Viborg on the Gulf of Finland across Stockholm and Bergslagen to Älvsborg on the west coast. Now, however, the main railway lines ran north/south, and that was that!

On Lake Mälar one could travel by steamboat. The first of these was "Amfitrie" which went into traffic in 1818. She was designed by the Englishman Samuel Owen and plied between Stockholm and Västerås/Uppsala.

Liberal reforms, 1840–1873

Swedish horizons broadened, but at the same time life became more complex. New professions and new communications demanded more and different forms of training and education.

This created the need for a school for the whole population, a *folkskola*. In 1842 an elementary education act was passed, prescribing that every parish should have at least one school.

Swedish women, who had always toiled along with the menfolk on the land, were considered inferior and undeserving of the right to inherit as much as the men. Then, following vehement debates in the Estates (male members only) it was decided in 1845, despite grave warnings as to the outcome, that daughters and sons should enjoy equal inheritence rights.

The following year, 1846, women were granted the right to run their own businesses. Shortly afterwards they were authorized to become elementary school teachers, which was approved by many of the tightfisted farmers who saw here the opportunity to keep the village teacher's wage at a minimum, since women were regarded as having "fewer demands on life".

In 1858 the Estates were ready for the next major reform after 50 years of discussion: unmarried women would come of age at 25 (men at 21). Women now went out into the business world.

With better techniques and improved equipment in agriculture the farmers had found themselves with money over. The first savings bank was thus opened in Göteborg in 1820 and from the 1830's onwards the banks began granting loans.

As industries grew in the mid-1800's the need arose for independent commercial banks and Swedish and foreign financiers recognized the scope for expansion in Sweden where there was an abundance of raw materials and plenty of cheap labour.

The first commercial bank, *Stockholms Enskilda Bank*, was opened by A.O. Wallenberg, closely followed by what is now *Skandinaviska banken* in Göteborg, founded by the German banker Mannheimer, and the German Fraenckel's *Handelsbanken* in Stockholm. These banking houses invested in new industries and in the export of timber and iron where Sweden became the main supplier in Europe.

The big currency reform took place in 1873 when Sweden went on the gold standard and the three Scandinavian countries introduced the *krona* and the *öre* in place of the *riksdaler*.

Meanwhile subversive movements in Europe, such as the February Revolution in Paris in 1848, had intensified the demands for political reforms in Sweden too.

The nobles and the monarchy opposed this for a long time, arguing that the Four Estates, which had existed since the Middle Ages, were a

On December 7, 1865, the representative assembly reform was introduced. By 381 votes to 284 the nobles surrendered their position of power. This cartoon by A.C. Wetterling illustrates the fate of the Four Estates.

Women also were now permitted to go into business. This little milliner's shop is a typical example.

The liberal reforms also resulted in improved national education, even though there were those who were critical of this. The bishop and poet Esaias Tegnér, for example, argued that all the common people required was a little instruction in religion, any other knowledge was "not only unessential but even harmful".

sound foundation for law and order. Discussions had been going on for more than sixty years and it was not until 1865 that a decision was finally reached. The Four Estates were to be dissolved and would be replaced by a bicameral *Riksdag*.

But Sweden was still a long way from full democracy since the vote for the Lower House was restricted to men, and then only those who were taxed for at least 800 *riksdaler* a year or owned property worth more than that. Thus from the outset the Lower House was dominated by the urban middle class and the wealthy farmers, while the working people and most of the rural population had no vote at all.

This unjust system whereby only 7 % of the population had any political influence created a vast, nation-wide movement which for half a century was to agitate for universal suffrage for both men and woman.

The mediaeval Four Estates had been supplanted by a new élitist system, but at the same time the elementary school and other liberal reforms created new, more self-assured groups which had become economically important to the country yet were denied any political influence. This situation in itself was a major threat to steady and stable development in the future.

The sawmill

At the top of the pile of timber we see Olof Näslund from Skönvik, near Sundsvall. His was the heaviest task of all in the succession of jobs from felling the trees in the forest to loading the sawn timber onboard ship for export. Olof Näslund had to stack the long, heavy, swaying planks in place so that they would dry and mature.

Sundsvall became the centre of world timber exports. Industrialism in Europe, especially Britain, greatly increased the demand for Swedish timber. Exports grew fivefold in 20 years. In 1870 more than 40 % of Sweden's exports were wood products and Sundsvall expanded at an unprecedented rate. People from practically all over Sweden, men, women and children, worked in the sawmills.

In Sweden industrialization began in the mid-1850's; a gradual, successive process. In certain areas, however, as for example around Sundsvall, things progressed very rapidly.

A series of factors contributed to this industrialization. Sweden was drawn into world economy at a time when she had plenty of cheap labour and venture capital, and when there was a widespread demand for such Swedish products as timber, tar, oats and iron.

The latest sawmills were driven by steam engines and could thus be built down at the harbourside where the sawn timber was stacked. Accommodation for all those who worked in the mill was provided nearby. There were soon so many sawmills that the poet Elias Sehlstedt wrote from Sundsvall in 1872: "And saw by saw I saw where ere I looked.

Business flourished and the sawmill owners soon began to invest in other products and other markets. It was now that the paper industry developed.

There was one fundamental difference between the Klondyke in the USA and Sundsvall's Klondyke, quite simply that no one who went to work in the Sundsvall mines returned home a millionaire.

On the other hand there are various similarities between Sweden in the middle of the last century and conditions in certain parts of south America today where the landless peasants are being drawn down to the coastal industries.

Like the other sawmill families, Olof Näslund and his family were granted "free housing" – one room, kitchen and larder – in the company's "barracks". This was crowded living to say the least; Näslund had ten children and sometimes had to make room as well for an extra worker.

In fact this free accommodation was not much of a concession considering the working conditions: twelve hours a day, six days a week, and often overtime. The pay was about 1 *riksdaler*, 50 *öre* an hour.

In the beginning the sawmill workers had not been paid at all. In-

The sawmill in Skönvik was owned by a German named Fredrik Bünsow who began his career working for a Stockholm publishing house before he moved on to Sundsvall and recognized the business scope of the timber industry. He bought up large areas of woodland and his company soon owned som 750 000 acres of forest, while the small sawmill expanded rapidly. Fredrik Bünsow became one of the most prominent of the "timber barons".

Fredrik and his wife Allona had a summer residence built, the Villa Merlo at Skönvik in the parish of Timrå. The photograph, right, shows a reconstruction of their dining room just before the arrival of supper guests. During the mill season, i.e. the summer, the Bünsow family lived at the Villa Merlo, but they spent the winters in Stockholm where they had a handsome house on prestigious Strandvägen.

Various other leading industrialists and sawmill owners who settled in Norrland and began their own businesses likewise came from abroad, among them the Dicksons from Scotland. Oscar Dickson lived not far from the Bünsows and ran the Svartvik sawmill. Other such families included the Carnegies and Gibsons. After the great fire in Sundsvall in 1888 the Bünsows came to live more permanently in Stockholm when their son took over the timber business.

In the simple abodes of the workers there was no room for luxury. The crowding was pitiful and often a family would have to sleep in shifts since there was not room enough for all to lie down at the same time.

stead they were given a chit valued at what they had earned and with this they could purchase whatever they needed in the company-owned store. A pair of shoes would cost 4 *riksdaler* or a woollen dress for the wife 12 *riksdaler*. The same system was in use recently in certain mines in southern Africa.

Näslund was permanently employed, which meant that his wife and children could also work at the sawmill. Right up until 1901 child labour was permitted, 12 to 14 hours a day, sometimes on the night shift. In the confined living conditions lice and disease were rife and many died of tuberculosis.

In Näslund's day the average length of life was about 40 years for men and 44 years for women. People were also stunted in growth, the average height of a 21-year old was little more than 165 cm, while today an 18-year old male Swede averages about 179 cm.

The emigrants

In the middle of the 19th century Swedes began to look to America. The first of those who made their way there did so in despair of the home country. They were liberals, members of the Free Church or abstainers, all protesting against Swedish conservatism.

They wanted to live in America, the land of the free where, they believed, everyone was equal and no one was harassed by officialdom, State church authorities and all the restraints and restrictions of Sweden.

Most of the first emigrants were disillusioned, however, and many of them returned disappointed. The next exodus began around the mid-1850's. These were largely landless farmhands and the sons of smallholders who hoped to be able to work their own farms in the new world. Many of them were successful and wrote home enthusiastically about their new lives. What became known as the "America fever" spread quickly, especially through the parishes of indigent Småland. This has been vividly and poignantly described in the epic novels of Vilhelm Moberg.

Two successive years of crop failure in the 1860's gave rise to another wave of emigration and in 1869 alone some 40 000 people quit Sweden. Around the end of the century most of the emigrants who left were from southwestern Sweden, but shortly after 1900 Swedes from the north, too, began to leave. About 75 % of these Swedish emigrants landed in New York before moving out across the continent. Many of them settled in the Chicago region or in Minnesota, while others spread out to various parts of the USA. Some emigrants went instead from Sweden to Australia.

This migration was something entirely new in Sweden's history. In the past the majority of Swedes had hardly been beyond their own parish but now, discouraged by hard times at home, tens of thousands set out in quest of a better life and greater opportunity elsewhere.

Between 1830 and 1930 over one million Swedes emigrated to America, which meant that by 1910 one Swede in five lived in the USA. They left their home country because they foresaw no future there. One wonders, meanwhile, what might have happened in Sweden if this million souls had not left the country. Would it then have been possible to avert the political explosion that was so close in 1917. Perhaps our revolution quite simply emigrated?

Ingeborg Jonsson, 17, on the America pier in Göteborg. Ingeborg was one of the ten children of an elementary school teacher from Köinge in Halland. She left in May, 1901, from Göteborg, like most of the immigrants. The first stage of the voyage was to Hull in England, then by train to Liverpool where the big Atlantic steamers waited.

The Swede Sven Winquist invented self-adjusting ballbearings on a basis of which he subsequently created the internationally-known company SKF.

Seven years before Henry Ford began assembly-line production of automobiles in the USA, Vagnsfabriks AB (Vabis) in Södertälje built Sweden's first paraffin-fuelled car, designed by Gustaf Eriksson 1897–98. This concern, later Scania-Vabis, began automobile production in 1901.

It was Johan P. Johansson who invented the adjustable spanner, or wrench; a universal tool today. He invented various other ingenious implements as well, for example the 3-pronged sugar tong.

Many of us today associate the factory chimney with pollution and death. But there was a time when this chimney was seen as a symbol of future prosperity and a better life for all.

Just as in China and North Korea today where factory chimneys belching black smoke are a popular motif in art, so at the beginning of this century Swedish poets penned ardent verses in praise of chimneys and the gleaming asphalt of industry. Factories and smoke represented development; progress.

The future, it was believed, lay in new, ingenious machines and never during such a short time as the few decades around the turn of the century did Swedes invent so many machines and devices for what later developed into multi-national concerns. Everyone is familiar with Alfred Nobel whose dynamite made him a multi-millionaire and resulted in the Nobel foundation with its world-famous annual awards.

But there were also many others who were busy at their drawing boards and in their laboratories. Gustaf Erik Pasch, for example, invented the safety match and in time Swedish safety match factories were built all round the world. And when our new industries exported their goods the ships could be guided through the dark and hazardous coastal waters thanks to Gustaf Dalén's acetylene gas light device which resulted in the AGA lighthouse. And again, modern space rockets are fitted with Laval-nozzles, invented once upon a time by Gustav de Laval.

In 1880 in the USA Thomas Alva Edison presented his incandescent lamp to an astonished world, while in fact a Swede named Jonas Wenström had already invented such a lamp. Edison was first out with his version, however. Wenström attained international recognition, nevertheless, by inventing such things as the electric motor and the generator or dynamo to produce electricity. This laid the ground for the development of such big concerns as ASEA, and Wenström became known as "the father of Swedish electronics".

There is a modern parallel to the companies built up around Swedish inventions: the Japanese miracle. Many of the large, well-known Japanese firms, like Sony and Hitaschi for example, were created after World War II thanks to the ideas of one man. The rapid technical development around Swedish inventions was in its day our "Japanese miracle".

How, meanwhile, have we handled this inheritance? Have we the capacity to do the same thing again?

Sweden and her associations

This is a typical example of a Swedish assembly hall anywhere in the country at the turn of the century.

Such a place was also in its way a sort of training establishment for Swedish democracy, for it was in buildings like this, here, there and everywhere in Sweden, that thousands of men and women congregated to discuss their common interests and concerns, to draw up the agenda for the evening's meeting and appoint a keeper of the minutes.

It was here that they discussed farming matters and here that lectures were delivered on travels to the Holy Land. God's word was preached and the people were warned of the perils of drunkenness. Here there were association festivities, and here last year's committee

The consumer association, Framtiden, *in Västanfors built its own little hall and this became the customary meeting place for all members.*

The sewing circles assembled in both large and small groups of skilled seamstresses who among other things contributed a great deal to relief work.

The association halls were the cradle of Swedish democracy. It was in such places that many of the men and women were trained and educated who would subsequently become instrumental in changing the structure of Swedish society. There were various social events here, too, and weddings.

was unanimously re-elected. Associations were formed for politics, temperance, religion, popular education and sports. These places were a hive of activity since it was now that new horizons were opened for the common people, things which had hitherto been denied the majority, especially those out in the rural areas. In associations like these, people who may never have enjoyed even an elementary education could take a course and learn a foreign language. They loaned each other books and studied subjects that many of them had never before heard of, everything from book-keeping to philosophy. They also learned how to organize a meeting and deliver a lecture. All this amounted to an introduction to democracy.

Swedish associations like these developed in time into powerful popular movements that were unique in Europe. First came the temperance movements and the Free Church while the political associations emerged a full generation later. The popular movements came at a time when the land-parcelling reform had reorganized the villages and the country as a whole was being transformed from an agrarian into an industrial society. This began a sort of general shift of the population when many left the land to work instead in industry. It was a time of profound change and new opportunity, yet most of the population were still not represented in the *Riksdag* and had little or no chance of a say in anything.

It was in these early assembly halls that many of the men and women were schooled who would later alter the entire social structure.

There was a distinct ideology behind all these movements, a vision of a new society. Even the sports organizations were of a patriotic and idealogical nature, stressing in particular the importance of character building.

As the industrial society developed the workers gradually became better organized, though this was a slow process. The first workers' associations were formed by the artisans and these were liberal. Union activities as such did not begin before the 1870's and here it was the big strike by the Sundsvall sawmill workers in 1879 which really set things moving.

The Social Democratic Party was founded in 1889, by which time the Farmers' or Country Party had already existed for two decades and there were eloquent liberals in the *Riksdag*. The Confederation of Trade Unions, LO, was set up in 1898 as a central organization for all the unions, but there still existed no legal right to form a union.

Whenever there was unrest the military were called in. Strikers were sacked and evicted from their homes and there were always several applicants for every available job. It took a long time to engender solidarity and a class feeling. Even as recently as the turn of the century only one Swedish workman in five belonged to a union and at that time the Social Democratic Party had barely 45 000 members.

THE WAR THAT NEVER WAS . . .

In the winter and spring of 1905 Swedish troops took up positions close along the Norwegian border, secret agents skulked around Norwegian military installations and Swedish intelligence registered pro-Swedish persons in Norway and anti-Swedish persons in Sweden. Meanwhile the General Staff put the final touches to its plans for an advance across the Norwegian frontier.

Was there to be war between Sweden and Norway?

Well, if it became necessary the Norwegians were apparently prepared to shoot their way out of the 1818 union which they had deeply resented from the outset. And Sweden, especially King Oscar II, was ready to shoot back to keep the Norwegians within the fold.

Norway's nationalism and the Norwegians' desire to assert themselves was understandable now in 1905, for Norway had, in fact, progressed more rapidly than Sweden. Industrialization had moved ahead more swiftly, the Norwegian merchant fleet had become one of the largest in the world, all Norwegian men had had the vote since 1898 and parliamentarism had been introduced ten years earlier.

Even as early as the 1880's there had been vociferous agitation in Norway against the union. The Norwegians were determined to go their own way; have their country to themselves. The dispute became acute when they demanded their own consulates abroad, complete with the Norwegian flag. Sweden was flatly opposed to this and the tension increased. Both sides began military preparations and in June 1905 Norway quite simply announced that the union had ceased to exist. This was regarded as an insult to Sweden and a personal affront to Oscar II. The situation deteriorated yet again when the Norwegians held a national referendum which showed total support for a free Norway. It was now that the Swedish military authorities prepared to issue the order "fix bayonets" and the Norwegians were ready to go into the trenches.

Fortunately, however, while all these military preparations were going on, negotiations had been begun in Karlstad between Norwegian and Swedish representatives. After three weeks of talks they reached an agreement and in October 1905 the union was peacefully dissolved, without a shot having been fired.

A neutral frontier zone was established between Norway and Sweden which was not finally abolished until 1993! By the terms of the agreement Norwegian frontier fortifications would be demolished and Swedish Lapps would have the right to graze their reindeer in northern Norway. During the negotiations the Norwegians had asked for a prince of the royal house of Bernadotte to become their king but in his chagrin Oscar II refused to go along with this. Instead Denmark's Prince Carl became king, as Haakon VII of Norway.

Preparations were made for war. Plans were drawn up for emergency food depots and similar contingencies. Field telegraphs and other such military equipment was made ready. But the crisis was finally settled peacefully.

The emergence of democracy

All too often during the course of Sweden's history there has been hardship, distress and hunger. Yet the people have always managed to handle these problems with fortitude and resourcefulness. They have assembled, discussed matters and done their best to find mutual solutions. And once decisions have been reached the majority have abided by them.

But in 1917 revolution came very close.

World War I had been raging for three long years. There was a revolution in Russia and Finland had gained her independence but was nevertheless on the brink of civil war. There was a state of dire unrest around Sweden's frontiers and here at home the situation was becoming increasingly critical. There was a serious shortage of food and daily reports of hunger riots all over the country. Workers fought with the police, grocery shops were looted and conscripted soldiers demonstrated in many of the towns, while the townspeople organized their own civil guard groups.

Hjalmar Branting laboured on amidst the political strife while unrest smouldered and a Swedish revolution threatened. But democracy was nevertheless attained by peaceful means. Universal suffrage was introduced and Branting's contribution here was of major importance.

In the leftwing fractions there were radicals who demanded swifter and more drastic action. They wanted a revolution. The Social Democratic Party was disrupted and a revolutionary group broke away altogether. Feelings were running so high at this time that on May Day even the SDP declared that "at times like this the working class should not hesitate for a moment to take to weapons if so needed. . ." Social Democrats returning from Russia spoke of "action now" and insisted that "our goals must be attained, using all and any means".

Many people wondered if there really would be a revolution. There were, after all, thousands upon thousands of starving, unemployed Swedes who had literally nothing to lose. During April 1917 there was almost daily rioting and tumult in one place or another. Many Social Democrats were clamouring for a republic, control of the industries by the workers and the expropriation of company property and large estates.

Others called for a general strike and the young socialists spoke exstatically of a proletarian dictatorship. Behind the scenes the SDP chairman Hjalmar Branting and the Federation of Swedish Trade Unions chairman Herman Lindqvist were doing what they could to appease the agitators, but the general feelings throughout the country and developments abroad frightened the government. The Social Democrats now seized the political initiative. In the autumn elections they were very successful, especially in their demands for universal suffrage, since at this time only 19 % of the population had the right to vote. The election results opened the way and the first Social Democrat ministers were able to take their place in the Liberal government.

During the winter and spring of 1918 there was bitter civil war in Finland and in November 1918 Germany collapsed and a wave of revolutionary ardour swept across Europe, central European monarchies disappeared and democratic constitutions were introduced. In Sweden activist workers demanded a republic, a unicameral parliament and universal suffrage. In this inflamed and increasingly threatening situation the Liberals and the Social Democrats reached an agreement which would finally give equal voting rights for both sexes in Sweden. This dramatically increased the size of the electorate; it had been 400 000 in 1905 and now it was over 3 million, or more than half the population. In the autumn of 1920 Hjalmar Branting formed Sweden's first Social Democratic government.

So there was no revolution in 1917 either. Perhaps primarily this was because Swedes had never in their history been involved in a real revolution; there was simply no tradition of revolution in this country. Discontent hade grown to breaking point, but because the SDP and the LO had managed to maintain some sort of control over most of their members and neither the police nor the military had lost their nerve and opened fire, the situation had been kept under control. But it was a close thing; as close as it has ever been in this country.

In 1909 a competition was announced for a national monument to be placed in front of the Riksdag building in Stockholm. The project was quickly abandoned, however, when Sven Boberg submitted his contribution: a Slumbering Mother Svea with the warrior kings Gustavus II Adolphus and Charles XII tucked down in the legs of her boots. Boberg named his work "Repose in Peace".

A new era was awaited; democracy was on its way; life would become more worthwhile. Here we have a good citizen on his way to welfare, hauling his belongings on a cart, away from overcrowding and outside privies to a modern apartment with bathroom and running water.

8
ARBETSDAG
ARBE
OCH
BRÖ

Accept this . . .

The 1930 Stockholm Exhibition was one of the most significant events in our modern history and it influenced considerably the everyday life of the country.

More than 4 million people attended the exhibition to learn what the future had to offer. And those who were in any doubt were encouraged by the exhibition slogan: "Accept this . . .". Never before had an exhibition so dramatically emphasized the future and dismissed the life styles and living conditions of the past.

The message was "What is practical is beautiful". This in effect was the creed of functionalism; a new mode introduced from Europe. It dismissed all the traditional "homely" knick-knacks and rejected heavy curtains across the windows. Now everything was to be bright, clean, smooth and useful.

Swedish people, for whom the kitchen had always been the nucleus of home life, would now move out into a living-room with standardized, series-produced furniture. No more massive, cumbersome fur-

No single exhibition has ever been as important to Sweden as the 1930 Stockholm Exhibition. It opened the door to a new era with new architecture and a new lifestyle. The man responsible for this exhibition, architect Gunnar Asplund, created a new concept for us: That which is simple and functional is beautiful.

nishings. In the new home each feature; chair, table, sofa and sideboard should have its own character and function, while the kitchen would be reduced to a mere workplace.

The ideas presented at the Stockholm Exhibition were immediately adopted by those who planned and designed housing. The great depression which had stricken the Western world around the turn of the 1930's had made it largely impossible to build houses and apartments as before, the solution now instead was economical, series-produced housing.

In the 1932 elections the Social Democrats, Communists and Farmers' Party triumphed. The leader of the SDP, Per Albin Hansson, became prime minister and, after bargaining with the Farmers' Party, in 1933 he was given a free hand to seek to implement his party's programme.

This was the beginning of Sweden's *Folkhem*, or Welfare Society, without class distinctions and where the strong would nurture the weak. Families with numerous children would be assured of assistance and given modern, functional housing, just as had been on show at the Stockholm Exhibition. From now on the interior of the home was no longer necessarily the business of those who lived there, instead it became a social and political matter.

A radical, progressive tax system was introduced to pay for the Welfare State and, according to the government, such a policy would also foster equality. In the foreign press this was described as "a Swedish revolution".

Not since Gustavus Vasa's time had Sweden undergone such an enormous change in her social structure, and various factors had facilitated this. One of the fundamental ingredients here was the economic boom which began in Sweden in the mid-1930's and continued almost without interruption until the close of the 1960's.

The labour market itself was stabilized in 1938 through an agreement on annual wage negotiations between LO, the Confederation of Trade Unions, and SAF, the Swedish Employers Confederation. There was widespread interest abroad in this agreement and Sweden became known as "the middle-way country"; an exemplary society.

Plans for new buildings were now not so much the business of the building companies' drawing offices as of the sociologists and social science experts. Their ambitions and results were based on statistics, social studies and a good helping of optimism and political ideology. They introduced reforms and drew up rules and regulations for a totally new way of living, thinking and working.

And the Swedish people, in any event the majority of them, did as they had customarily done through history – they accepted this. They moved out to the new suburbs, sat back in their new living rooms and reflected that this idea of the practical and the functional was probably a pretty good thing altogether!

Neutrality

On September 1, 1939, Germany invaded Poland and World War II had begun. The day before, Sweden's prime minister had announced that Sweden was "in a good state of readiness". That was a gross exaggeration. Our military defence organization was too small, it was poorly equipped and it had never been trained for warfare.

Sweden now formed a coalition government and proclaimed herself neutral in the war, arming at the same time for whatever might happen. Then when Russia attacked Finland in November 1939 Sweden declared that she was "non-biligerent" and Finland was left to fight the 100-day winter war on her own. The newly formed Swedish government sent weapons, ammunition and humanitarian aid and many Swedes went to the Finnish front as volunteers. Meanwhile the refugees began to arrive.

Sweden remained neutral during World War II, though with certain loopholes. We sold iron ore to Germany and thereby avoided invasion. Our state of readiness, however, was far from what it was claimed to be. When Germany invaded Denmark and Norway, Sweden mobilized and the psychological defence authorities urged the people to hold their tongues, stressing that the enemy was always listening. A great many refugees fled to Sweden but for the average Swede the war was no more than something one saw on films and read about in the newspapers.

Not before April 9 when Germany attacked Denmark and Norway and war threatened her frontiers did Sweden mobilize. Within a few weeks 320 000 men had been called in and Swedes were standing guard around the clock along the frontiers and out in the east coast archipelago. In the southwest one could see the Germans across the Öresund while in the north towns were ablaze within the Finnish border. The odd aircraft flew in over Sweden and once or twice bombs were dropped by mistake on Swedish territory. Danish and Norwegian resistance fighters came to Sweden seeking assistance and refugees arrived from the Baltic states and the other Nordic countries.

Civil defence was built up and the Home Guard organized. The voluntary rifle brigades trained thousands of people. Generally speaking

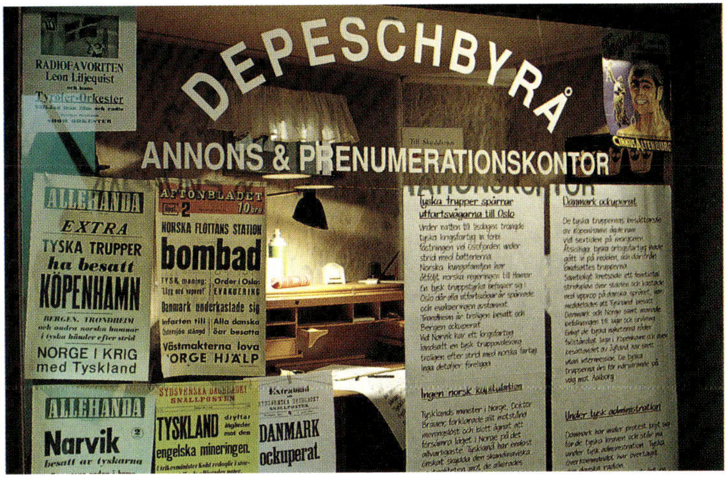

the government managed to organize emergency supplies, but the main problem was a shortage of fuel. Vehicles ran on producer-gas and in farms and gardens logs were cut and stacked.

The psychological defence authorities were at work 24 hours a day, using press, radio, films and even popular songs. But Sweden failed to intervene militarily to help her neighbours and the majority of Swedes had little experience of the war beyond what they saw on newsreels and read in the papers.

Sweden was neutral, though just as during World War I, with certain provisoes. We continued to export iron ore to Germany in order to secure in return coal, coke, fertilizers and other vital commodities. This was not necessarily interpreted as a breach of neutrality – but something else quite definitely was: between June 1940 and August 1943 over 2 million troops passed through Sweden from Germany and Norway and the so-called Engelbrekt division was permitted transit from southern Norway to northern Finland.

Staying out of the war and managing on our own engendered a foreign policy and a general attitude to the outside world which was to characterize Sweden for another 50 years or more. It was thus not until the 1990's that it became politically acceptable even to question the policy of neutrality. Only then could the political establishment, without risk of political suicide, discuss Sweden's political association with other countries.

There was nothing admirable about the appeasement policy of the war years, it brought no medals, no wreaths were placed at the foot of war memorials or cenotaphs, and when our Nordic neighbours and others tell of the trials and horrors of the war, the Swede keeps quiet.

But for better or for worse this appeasement policy brought the Swedish people safely through the European holocaust.

The Swedish model, 1950's & 1960's

Peace came in May 1945. While Europe lay in ashes and ruin with millions dead and maimed, the Swedes could quickly resume a normal, peaceful way of life in a country where nothing at all had been destroyed or wasted. The wartime coalition was promptly dissolved and the Social Democrats returned to, and remained in power for 22 years – a western European record.

We joined the newly-founded United Nations but when the political climate hardened and the cold war began we stayed out of things, just as we steered clear of the trade blocs which had begun to form in Europe.

We had our engineering plants, we had our hydro-electric power, our timber and our ore. Sweden was very quickly on her feet again and soon passed her competitors on the world markets and in international trade figures.

Never before in our modern history had we experienced such expansion. It was as though we were recovering our status as a great power. On Swedish ballbearings Swedish quality rolled out across the world while such things as Japanese electronics and Brazilian steel were still unheard of. Swedish-made artillery guarded borders and frontiers everywhere. Swedish telephone systems were installed in new

Driving school in the 1950's.

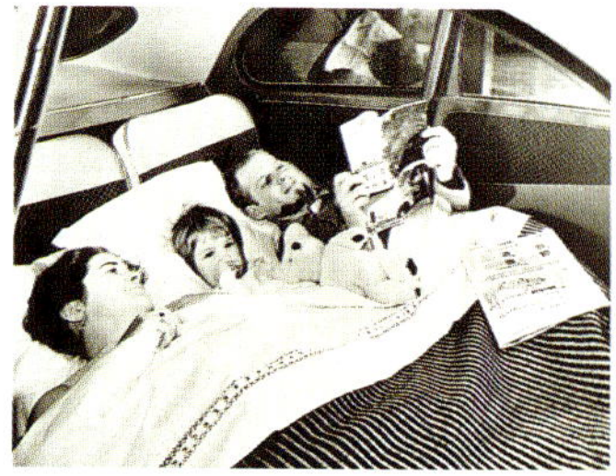

The ultimate holiday dream for Swedes was fulfilled with the "bedable" SAAB automobile.

The "gadget craze" came with the new age of plastics in the 1950's and '60's.

SAAB 1955-56

capitals. Dag Hammarskjöld became head of the UN. Most Swedes were, in fact, quite satisfied that their country was just that "dreamland" which the foreign media wrote of: the Swedish Model.

The development of the Welfare State and "social engineering" continued. Just as during the 17th century great power era, Sweden's towns were again modernized, with the tearing down and rebuilding of entire blocks. Where there had formerly been a church and the offices of royal officials there was now a department store, a multi-storey carpark and a social centre. This was a time of new values and new ideals.

Where people had once dreamed of recreation and holidays they were now encountering the problem of what to do with their spare time. Where they had once socialized at the church they now wandered about the shopping centres, waiting for the evening's television programme to begin.

The USA had won the war and then she began the conquest of western Europe and Sweden. The great American dream which still prevails as a young people's cult; future prospects, success and the gadget craze.

At this time in Sweden it seemed that each year could only be better than the preceding one. Wages increased steadily and the future looked good. There were far more jobs than could be filled, so that companies had to recruit their manpower abroad; first in the neighbouring countries and then farther and farther afield.

Growing incomes provided more taxes for even more extensive reform programmes, since everyone was convinced that next year would be even better. The national pensions scheme was the essence of this philosophy where it was reckoned that each new generation would be better off than the previous one and would thus be able to finance the pensions of future generations. Unemployment and wage cuts were unthinkable. With each election the government's protective net was drawn more securely over the Welfare State; a net which may have made Sweden unique in a way but tended perhaps at the same time to inhibit our insight into and understanding of the outside world. Compliance; acquiescence, was the password. Anyone who thought otherwise was a reactionary.

More and more people moved in from the countryside and what had previously been over 2 000 independent towns was condensed into barely 300 "communes", i.e. municipal districts. The Swedish people became wage-earners in the public sector or private concerns and the rural homes of their childhood weekend and holiday retreats.

But then one day, all of a sudden, the world caught up with Sweden. We did not win as many medals anymore, new nations appeared on the Olympics prize-stands and countries we scarcely knew the whereabouts of passed on ahead of us in world trade statistics. The great awakening was at hand.

THE AWAKENING, SWEDEN AND THE WORLD

In 1968 the world entered our living rooms. On our television screens we saw barricades being raised in the streets of Paris. Soviet tanks rumbled into Prague. Bombs fell over Indochina. The students in Stockholm stormed the student union building. Thousands of young people demonstrated in Europe and the USA. A wave of leftwing sentiment swept through most parliaments as socialism of every conceivable shade flourished. To demonstrate was to care.

Sitting at our breakfast tables we suddenly become aware that what goes on in other countries affects Sweden too. Vietnam, the student revolt in Paris, the murder of Olof Palme, the fall of the Berlin Wall, new influxes of refugees; everything happening around the world reaches us swiftly and with stunning clarity.

In Swedish industries there were wildcat strikes. People sat at their kitchen tables in the suburbs and discussed the military junta in Chile and the regime in Rhodesia. Sweden had suddenly become part of the world; an interested and active party who decided in 1968 that her foreign aid to the developing countries should be at least 1 % of the GNP.

The world quailed beneath the shadow of the cold war. The numbers of nuclear warheads multiplied on both sides in increasingly complex and advanced weapon systems. Around the clock the military sat at their screens, ready to press their buttons and destroy the world.

The first warnings of impoverishment and environmental pollution came in the 1960's but these were derisively dismissed as alarmism and doomsday pessimism. Not until around the early 1970's, however, did we realize that the party really was coming to an end. OPEC steeply increased its oil prices. Gasolene, electricity and regional hot water was rationed in Sweden and the entire question of our energy supplies was seriously debated. The nuclear power plant scare at Three Mile Island in the USA was effectively used by the anti-nuclear power movements here, so that in a referendum shortly afterwards the majority voted against the expansion of Sweden's nuclear power programme.

The UN held its big environmental conference in Stockholm in 1972. People now became much more aware of the threat to the environment as month after month new studies and reports made us appreciate the folly of our consumer use and discard attitude.

In 1986 Prime Minister Olof Palme was shot to death on the street in Stockholm, making us realize abruptly and brutally that political violence could strike even here in the midst of all our secureness and self-assurance.

Nothing was the same anymore, neither here at home nor out in the world. Old precepts no longer applied. Past enemies were shaking hands. US and Soviet heads of government signed disarmament agreements. Political systems which had endured for decades were destroyed overnight. Europe's iron curtain disintegrated. Dictator regimes collapsed. Countries and cities were renamed and Sweden acquired new neighbours. Old alliances were dissolved and new ones formed.

European frontiers began to disappear. A new community was emerging, the European Union, so that 300 million West Europeans would be able to live and work in a frontierless Europe. At the same time more mined and barbed-wire barriers were being raised amidst pitiless warring in other parts of Europe.

Today Sweden is a nation of many languages and many cultures. She has over one million immigrants or descendants of immigrants and by the year 2000 every other baby will be an "immigrant child". Even in our kitchens there are different aromas from grandmother's day, door-plates show strange names while television and radio programmes are dominated by American music and entertainment. At our Lucia festival we pay homage to a Sicilian saint, while our Christmas customs have come mainly from Germany. We listen to songs by Taube whose ancestors came from the Baltic states, or Bellman whose grandfather was German, while other popular melodies have originated in South America and Europe.

Without the import of raw materials and the export of her own products Sweden would come to a standstill. In fact Sweden has never really been isolated, having from her very beginnings had contacts in one form or another with the world around her.

Throughout our history we have found inspiration in the big changes which have taken place elsewhere. We have learned from all this and utilized it for our own purposes. One might say that the world is here and we are out there in the world, through our products but also through the ideas and incentives which our films, our artists, our athletes, our expatriots and our UN soldiers for peace are spreading beyond our own borders.

This then has been our journey through history. This is why we are here at this moment, why we are called what we are and look as we do. Yesterday is history. Tomorrow is the future.

Where do we go from here?

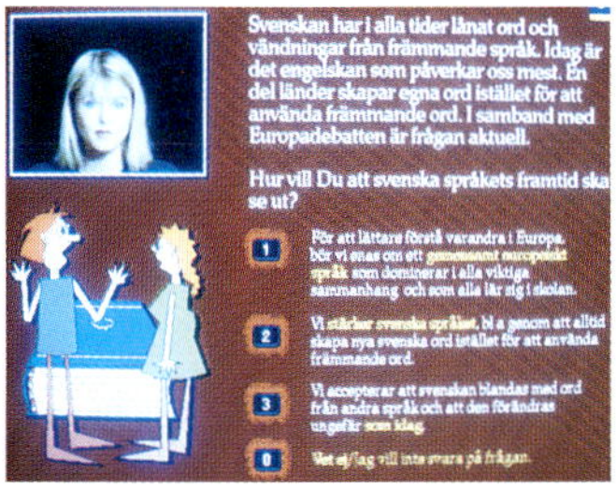

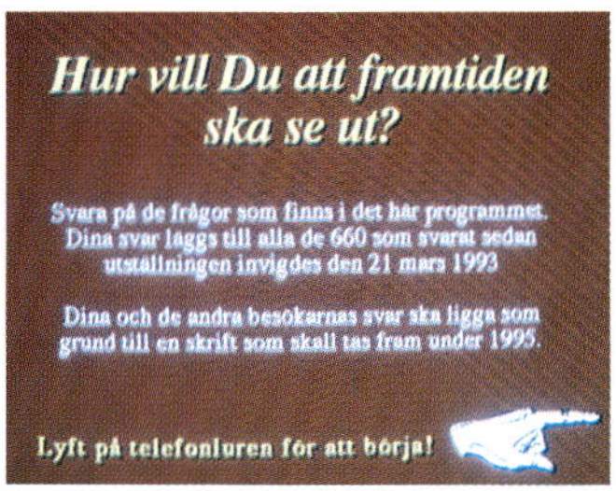

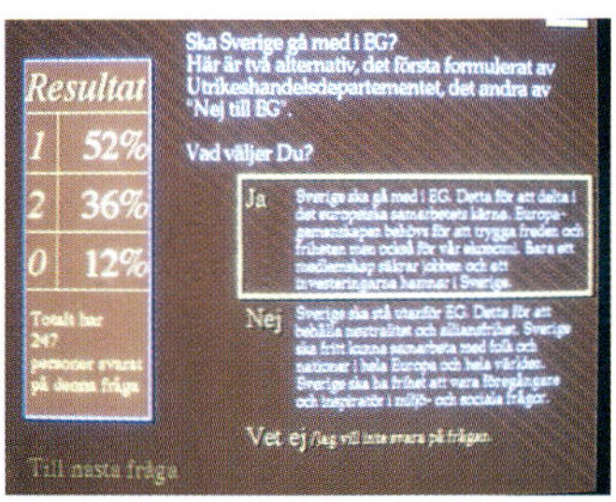

What do we want of our future? How can we influence it? Through computer technology we can quickly make ourselves heard wherever we wish, we can produce statistics and analyses, we can make choices, answer questions and make proposals – on child welfare, refugee policy, schooling, the working environment. So what will Swedish history look like in the future?

All photographs by
Sören Hallgren and Peter Segermark
except
p. 23 Bibliothèque Nationale, Paris
p. 29 Gösta Glase
p. 30 Linköping treasure, Gunnel Jansson
p. 59 Linné, p. 86 Immigrant family, Mats Landin

Scene from 30-Years War, pp 42–43
based on an illustration by Björn Gidstam

Scene from the Dalecarlian insurrection, p. 56
from the original painting by Göte Göransson

Figures on pp. 27, 49, 50, 65 & 79
by Eva Rahmqvist and the Gunilla
and Rune Vidstige workshop

Silhouette p. 61 from the shadow-play
"Death at the Opera" by the Marionette
Theatre Group

Cover illustration:
Carl Wahlbom: Death of Gustavus II Adolphus
at Lützen
NATIONAL MUSEUM, STOCKHOLM

EDITOR: GIL DAHLSTRÖM
GRAPHIC LAYOUT: ARNE ÖSTRÖM

TRANSLATION: ALAN TAPSELL

ISBN 91-7119-705-2

PRINTED IN DENMARK 1994